# The Algorithmic Edge

# The Algorithmic Edge

## Outsmarting the Market with AI and Data

Adrian Colehart

Mindful Pages

Published in 2025

ISBN: 9789371779289 (PB)
ISBN: 9789371771825 (eBook)

*Published by*

**Mindful Pages**
*Imprint of Alpha Editions LLC*
312 W. 2nd St #1834
Casper, WY 82601, USA



This book was developed using advanced writing tools to support the drafting and ideation process. All content has been thoughtfully curated, refined, and reviewed to ensure quality and relevance.

# Content

# Introduction
# The New Playbook for the Retail Investor

For decades, the sharpest tools in the financial markets were shrouded in secrecy. Algorithmic trading systems—crafted by teams of mathematicians, computer scientists, and seasoned market operators—functioned in closed environments, accessible only to the most well-resourced hedge funds and proprietary trading firms. These programmes could process torrents of market data in milliseconds, execute trades with precision, and capitalise on opportunities that would vanish before any human could react. To the average investor, such systems were almost alchemical in their mystique.

That era of exclusivity, however, has passed. The computational power that once demanded entire trading floors now fits on a consumer laptop. Cloud platforms stream live market data to anyone with a broadband connection, and machine learning frameworks—once the domain of specialists—are now wrapped in interfaces that even a novice can navigate. What was once jealously guarded knowledge is, in principle, available to anyone willing to learn how to use it.

Yet access does not equate to mastery. Many retail investors remain paralysed by intimidation, believing "quant" tools are beyond comprehension, or overconfident, assuming that access alone confers expertise. The outcome is predictable: algorithms are underutilised by those who could benefit most, and misapplied by those least equipped to understand their constraints. The promise of democratised finance, despite its potential, remains largely unrealised.

This book seeks to change that. It does not offer a magic formula or a shortcut to effortless wealth. It does not portray algorithms as omniscient entities. Instead, it provides something far more valuable: a structured, repeatable framework for blending algorithmic insight with human judgment. The goal is not to replace the investor but to augment them—to leverage the precision, speed, and consistency of machines while retaining the context, adaptability, and ethical discernment that only humans can provide.

The need for this balance has never been greater. Markets are more complex and faster than ever before. Price movements are influenced not just by earnings or economic reports, but by high-frequency trading, global sentiment swings, geopolitical shocks, and the constant chatter of social media. Information no longer travels at a human pace. Those relying solely on intuition or traditional news cycles are effectively competing in a different game—one where opponents move faster, armed with far more data.

By the end of this book, you will know how to construct and operate what I call your decision engine: a disciplined system in which algorithms identify opportunities and risks, while you determine how and when to act. You will learn to strip away the noise, focus on signals that matter, and test ideas safely. You will develop guardrails to protect against both market volatility and your own behavioural pitfalls. And you will do all this without learning to code, decoding complex mathematics, or subscribing to opaque, expensive platforms.

The stakes extend beyond mere finances. Retail traders often oscillate between panic and overconfidence, chasing trends in moments of euphoria and freezing under uncertainty. Algorithms, when correctly applied, can serve as a stabilising force—enforcing rules when emotions urge deviation, revealing opportunities that intuition alone would miss.

But clarity is essential. Algorithms are not fortune tellers. They do not "know" the future. They process data, identify patterns, and execute instructions with unwavering obedience, regardless of whether those rules are sound or flawed. They will not alert you when your assumptions are outdated; interpretation and adjustment remain firmly human responsibilities.

This book begins by dismantling the myth of the infallible machine, explaining how algorithms evolved from secret institutional weapons to off-the-shelf platforms, and why their reputation for omniscience is overstated. We will explore how algorithms perceive the market differently from humans, detecting patterns beyond our perception and filtering noise with unmatched consistency.

From there, we move to practical construction: defining objectives, structuring rule-based strategies, and avoiding pitfalls such as overfitting, where a strategy is perfectly tuned to past data but fails in the future. You will learn to integrate human judgment with algorithmic output, building a workflow where both play to their strengths.

We will also examine the retail AI marketplace, navigating overhyped platforms, unverified claims, and scams. You will learn to separate credible tools from predatory ones, testing strategies safely before committing capital.

Once theory translates into practice, we will establish guardrails: position sizing, stop-loss protocols, diversification, and automated safeguards. And we will confront the most insidious threat of all: human psychology. Biases do not vanish when algorithms are adopted; they migrate into the code or manifest in interpretation. Learning to identify and correct these distortions is as crucial as refining the algorithms themselves.

Finally, you will learn to scale your system responsibly, adapt to shifting market conditions, and maintain an edge without chasing every new tool or trend. The aim is not to win every trade or maximise short-term returns, but to build a sustainable, resilient process—one that outperforms the average trader through discipline and intelligent application of available tools.

If you are reading this, you already sense that the modern market favours those adept at leveraging technology. You are correct. Yet technology alone is insufficient. The true advantage lies in knowing when to trust the machine, when to trust yourself, and how to create a process that fuses the strengths of both.

This is the new playbook for the retail investor. Not the old game of chasing tips, blind momentum, or gut instinct. Not the fantasy of autonomous trading that prints money while you sleep. Rather, it is a considered, practical approach: recognising algorithms as powerful allies that, when guided with skill and awareness, extend your capacity to perceive and act in the market.

What follows is not abstract theory or principle. It is a field manual for intelligent investing in the algorithmic age—grounded in evidence, tested in practice, and shaped by the realities of human behaviour. Commit to the process, and you will sharpen not only your financial results but your ability to think clearly and act decisively amid uncertainty.

The door is open. The tools are at your disposal. Now it is time to learn how to wield them.

# Chapter 1
# The Myth of the Machine Genius

For much of modern financial history, algorithms were whispered about with the reverence reserved for classified weapons: precise, formidable, and jealously protected. On Wall Street, the earliest adopters were proprietary trading desks and quantitative hedge funds capable of financing both the computational infrastructure and the rarefied talent needed to construct these systems. In the 1980s and 1990s, firms such as Renaissance Technologies, D.E. Shaw, and specialised trading units at Goldman Sachs poured millions into building proprietary models. These systems could sift through staggering volumes of market data, detect fleeting inefficiencies, and execute trades faster than any human reflex could manage. They were not side projects—they were fortresses of technology, safeguarded not merely by firewalls but by secrecy, non-compete clauses, and a talent pipeline that recruited only the most elite mathematicians and computer scientists. For outsiders, the notion of accessing such tools was as fanciful as running a personal satellite network.

The exclusivity, however, rested not solely on cost or hardware; it was equally a matter of expertise. Early algorithms were dense mathematical constructs requiring years of specialised study to comprehend. Even if one gained access to the code, operating it effectively was a challenge entirely unto itself. This gave rise to a mystique: these systems were perceived as possessing near-supernatural insight into market movements, and their creators as members of a financial priesthood. The aura was intensified by the industry's opacity—few firms explained their methods, fewer still admitted failures.

Gradually, the fortress began to erode—not because the insiders grew generous, but because technology advanced, costs declined, and knowledge became more widely available. The advent of personal computing in the 1990s, the broadband boom of the 2000s, and the proliferation of open-source software in the 2010s chipped away at the barriers. Platforms like MetaTrader, QuantConnect, and TradeStation offered retail traders the ability to backtest strategies, access market data, and automate trade execution without constructing systems from scratch. Cloud computing allowed anyone with a modest subscription to rent the processing power once reserved for entire server rooms. Machine learning libraries such as TensorFlow and PyTorch—initially developed for academic or industrial research—became freely accessible, enabling even non-specialists to experiment with predictive models.

Despite this democratisation, the myth of exclusivity lingers. Partly, it survives through inertia: old narratives die slowly, particularly when they serve the interests of those who prospered from the opacity. Partly, it is intimidation: while access is easier, mastery remains challenging, and the complexity of these systems can feel alien to those without a quantitative background. Partly, it is marketing: fintech, like any industry, thrives on mystique, and vendors are keen to imply their tools contain a spark of genius unattainable elsewhere. The danger lies in these myths—they either deter potential users entirely or entice them into uncritical adoption, both of which can lead to poor outcomes.

Here, a fundamental truth must be stated: algorithms are not magic bullets. At their core, they are rule-based systems designed to process inputs and produce outputs. They excel at certain tasks—detecting subtle correlations, enforcing discipline in trade execution, eliminating hesitation—but their effectiveness depends entirely on the quality of the data and the logic upon which they are built. Blind faith in an algorithm is as perilous as blind faith in a human tipster. Consider Knight Capital Group's $440 million loss in 45 minutes in 2012: it was not the market turning cruelly, but a software deployment error unleashing errant orders faster than anyone could respond. The 2010 "Flash Crash" similarly revealed how algorithms, acting in concert, can amplify volatility within minutes, producing dramatic swings before stabilisation. These episodes demonstrate that speed and complexity can magnify errors just as efficiently as profits.

Even perfectly executed code can falter if its assumptions are flawed. A model designed for a trending market can lose heavily in sideways conditions. An algorithm trained on bullish data may misinterpret signals in a downturn. Data appearing flawless in backtests can prove incomplete, biased, or irrelevant under new circumstances. Simply put, algorithms are only as good as the thought and oversight that govern them.

Human bias, too, often infiltrates supposedly objective systems. We might select datasets confirming pre-existing views, choose parameters flattering past performance, or interpret ambiguous outputs in line with hopes rather than probabilities. In extreme cases, we anthropomorphise the system, attributing "insight" or "intent" to deterministic processes. Left unchecked, these biases erode performance and undermine the very discipline algorithms aim to enforce.

Thus, the principle of "trust, but verify" is central. Trust is required—interfering mid-execution can ruin automated advantages—but verification is indispensable. This entails monitoring performance, testing assumptions, stress-testing under adverse scenarios, and being willing to deactivate a model when it no longer meets purpose. Treat the algorithm as a highly skilled assistant: capable, consistent, and fast, but never as an oracle.

In this chapter, we dismantle the myth of the machine genius, tracing the journey of algorithms from the exclusive arsenals of Wall Street to the hands of ordinary investors. We examine why mystique persists, even as the mechanics become transparent, and explore how human flaws can infiltrate ostensibly objective code. Above all, we establish the mental framework for the book: human judgment and machine execution in partnership, reinforcing one another, never left unchecked.

By the end, you will see algorithms in their proper light: as tools of immense potential, yet not omniscient; as allies for disciplined, evidence-based decision-making, yet never substitutes for human responsibility to think, question, and adapt. Stripping away the illusion of machine genius is the first step to using these tools as they were always meant to be used: not as magic, but as method.

## From Wall Street's Secret Weapon to Public Tool

The first generation of trading algorithms were conceived not as conveniences for the everyday investor, but as competitive weapons in a highly exclusive arms race. In the 1970s and 1980s, Wall Street's most forward-thinking firms began to experiment with computer-assisted order execution, aiming to shave fractions of a second off trade placement and to manage large block orders without moving market prices unfavourably. These early systems were crude by today's standards, but they required resources, infrastructure, and technical expertise that only the largest investment houses could marshal. Access was tightly controlled, and the algorithms themselves—developed by small teams of quants with backgrounds in mathematics, physics, and computer science—were guarded as intellectual property on par with corporate secrets. The public, and even most of the finance industry, had little idea these tools existed.

By the 1990s, as computing power increased and data became more granular, the scope of these systems expanded. The rise of electronic communication networks (ECNs) allowed institutions to match buyers and sellers directly, bypassing traditional exchanges for faster execution. High-frequency trading (HFT) emerged, driven by algorithms capable of analysing market data and executing trades in milliseconds. Firms such as Renaissance Technologies and D.E. Shaw became legendary for their secrecy and consistent returns, while investment banks developed proprietary platforms that integrated execution algorithms into their trading desks. This was the "closed shop" era: algorithms existed behind layers of firewalls, inaccessible to outsiders, with their very design premised on keeping the edge to as few players as possible. For the retail investor, the market remained a slower, more opaque place, shaped by human brokers, delayed quotes, and trading fees that discouraged frequent adjustments.

Two forces began to undermine this exclusivity. First, technology costs fell precipitously. The processing power once requiring an entire data centre could be purchased in the form of an off-the-shelf server, or eventually rented on demand through cloud services. Second, the internet dramatically expanded the flow of information. As exchanges digitised and regulatory changes opened up more market data, enterprising developers outside the institutional sphere began to experiment with tools that mirrored, on a smaller scale, what the big firms had been using for years. In the late 1990s and early 2000s, retail trading platforms such as TradeStation and MetaTrader introduced features for strategy backtesting and automated execution, allowing non-professionals to create simple rule-based trading systems without writing complex code from scratch. This was the first meaningful crack in the wall.

The cultural shift accelerated with the open-source movement. Libraries for statistical analysis and machine learning, once confined to academic research or corporate labs, became freely downloadable. Python, R, and later JavaScript-based tools offered accessible gateways into data manipulation and modelling. QuantConnect and Quantopian built communities around crowd-sourced algorithm design, hosting competitions where users could submit strategies and see how they performed against historical data. The idea that algorithmic trading was the sole domain of elite hedge funds began to erode—not because the underlying complexity had diminished, but because the tools to engage with it had multiplied and simplified.

Yet the myth of exclusivity endured. Part of this is because access does not equate to advantage. Many retail traders discovered that the leap from running a backtest to making consistent real-world profits was far greater than anticipated. Institutional players still held advantages in data speed, market access, and capital deployment. They could afford co-location—placing their servers physically close to exchange infrastructure to reduce latency by microseconds—something well beyond the reach of the average investor. They could negotiate lower trading fees, tap into alternative data sources, and employ teams to continually refine models. Even as the *capabilities* of algorithms spread, the *edge* they delivered at the institutional level remained formidable.

The persistence of the machine mystique is also reinforced by the opacity of the most successful strategies. Renaissance Technologies' Medallion Fund, often cited as the pinnacle of quantitative performance, is closed to outside investors and reveals nothing of its internal workings. When the public sees consistent outperformance without a clear explanation, it is tempting to attribute it to some hidden genius in the machine. Vendors of retail trading software have capitalised on this perception, often marketing their platforms with vague promises of "institutional-grade" intelligence, encouraging the belief that simply possessing the tool is enough to replicate institutional success.

What is often overlooked in this narrative is the role of regulatory change in widening access. The introduction of the Regulation National Market System (Reg NMS) in the United States in 2005 increased competition among exchanges and facilitated electronic trading. In Europe, the Markets in Financial Instruments Directive (MiFID) opened markets and fostered innovation in execution services. These policy shifts, combined with technological progress, brought previously fragmented liquidity and data streams into more accessible formats. While the retail trader still lacked the sheer scale of institutional operations, they could now plug into a far richer and faster market ecosystem than at any point in history.

It would be misleading, however, to suggest that this democratisation is complete. The barriers have shifted rather than disappeared. Today's retail investor faces a subtler challenge: information overload. Where once the problem was a lack of access, now it is the abundance of tools, platforms, and data streams—many of them poorly vetted, mis-sold, or overcomplicated. The mere presence of algorithmic capability does not guarantee competence in its use. Understanding how to select, test, and adapt an algorithm to shifting market conditions remains as critical as in the days when these systems were locked inside institutional vaults.

Historical perspective helps to anchor this point. Consider the analogy of navigation. For centuries, only trained navigators with access to charts, sextants, and maritime experience could guide ships across oceans. The arrival of GPS made navigation accessible to anyone with a handheld device, but it did not eliminate the possibility of error, nor did it replace the judgment required to respond to unexpected conditions. Similarly, the transition from algorithmic exclusivity to mass availability has given many more people the ability to "plot a course" in the markets, but it has not removed the skill element—or the capacity for self-deception. The navigator who blindly trusts a malfunctioning GPS can run aground just as quickly as a sailor misreading the stars.

The lesson, therefore, is that the real shift is not merely technological but cultural. What was once a secretive, high-cost capability has entered the public sphere, but the responsibility for intelligent use rests squarely on the individual. For the thoughtful retail investor, this is both an opportunity and a test. The opportunity lies in the fact that the tools to analyse, automate, and execute strategies are no longer the preserve of a few. The test lies in developing the discernment to separate genuine capability from marketing gloss, and in building the discipline to operate these tools within a coherent, evidence-based investment process.

The journey from Wall Street's secret weapon to public tool is not a story of the machine becoming inherently smarter—it is a story of distribution, adaptation, and the slow erosion of structural advantages. It is also a reminder that access is not the same as mastery, and that the myth of exclusivity often lingers because it contains a kernel of truth: those who wield the tools with deeper understanding and greater discipline will continue to outperform those who mistake possession for proficiency. The algorithms have been set loose into the wild, but the craft of using them wisely remains, as ever, the true differentiator.

### Why Algorithms Aren't Magic Bullets

The belief that algorithms can outthink, outmanoeuvre, and outlast the market is as persistent as it is seductive. It rests on the notion that complexity equals superiority—that the sheer mathematical depth of a model somehow guarantees its success. Yet financial history offers no shortage of examples in which sophisticated algorithms, entrusted with enormous sums of capital, have failed spectacularly. The lesson is not that these systems are inherently flawed, but that they are only as sound as the assumptions, data, and oversight that govern them. To treat an algorithm as a flawless oracle is to mistake a tool for an inevitability.

The Knight Capital disaster of 2012 is perhaps the most striking modern cautionary tale. A leading market-making firm at the time, Knight deployed new trading software intended to handle order execution across multiple securities. Within minutes of the system going live, a coding error began sending a torrent of unintended orders into the market. Automated processes executed them without hesitation or human review, accumulating a massive and unwanted position in a matter of seconds. By the time the error was identified and the system shut down, the firm had lost $440 million—enough to nearly collapse the business. What is striking is not just the magnitude of the loss, but the speed: in less than three-quarters of an hour, a technical oversight had undone decades of operational credibility. The problem was not that the algorithm "malfunctioned" in a sentient sense, but that it executed precisely what it had been instructed to do, without any awareness of the broader consequences.

Equally illustrative is the "Flash Crash" of 6 May 2010, when the Dow Jones Industrial Average plunged nearly 1,000 points in minutes, erasing almost $1 trillion in market value before rebounding. Investigations revealed a confluence of factors—one large sell order, fragmented liquidity, and the rapid interplay of high-frequency trading algorithms reacting to one another in a feedback loop. The machines were not behaving irrationally according to their internal logic; they were simply responding to price movements with pre-programmed rules that, in aggregate, amplified volatility beyond anything human traders could have engineered in such a short period. This was not a system breakdown in the traditional sense. It was the unintended consequence of many algorithms following their own incentives without a central mechanism for moderation.

These events underscore a critical point: *algorithms are deterministic*. They do not improvise, second-guess, or pause to consider whether market conditions have deviated from expectations. They execute code against input data, relentlessly and consistently. This is a strength when the data is relevant and the rules are well-designed; it is a weakness when either is flawed. A backtest that looks impeccable on a decade's worth of historical data may still fail catastrophically in live conditions if the underlying market regime shifts. The global financial crisis of 2008 is an example of a regime change that invalidated many quantitative models built on assumptions of market stability and liquidity. Models that priced mortgage-backed securities as low-risk instruments based on decades of housing data were blindsided when the foundational premise—that national housing prices would not decline significantly—collapsed.

The problem is compounded by the fact that financial data is not a neutral record of the world. It is generated in an environment shaped by human behaviour, policy decisions, and evolving market structures. An algorithm trained on data from a period of low volatility will learn patterns that may not survive in a high-volatility regime. Similarly, a system optimised for a bull market may misinterpret the signals of a downturn, not because it is "wrong" in a technical sense, but because the environment it was optimised for no longer exists. This is the fragility of overfitting—the tendency to create a model so finely tuned to past conditions that it fails in the face of new realities.

Blind trust in automation also overlooks a subtler limitation: algorithms cannot distinguish between a data anomaly and a genuine market signal unless explicitly programmed to do so. In August 2012, trading in several U.S. stocks was temporarily halted after a flood of erroneous orders from an automated system disrupted pricing. The system had no mechanism for self-audit beyond the execution layer; it assumed all inputs were valid. Without human intervention, such anomalies can propagate unchecked, distorting prices and triggering further automated responses.

This is why effective algorithmic trading demands a layered approach to oversight. First, there must be rigorous pre-deployment testing across diverse market conditions, including stress scenarios designed to simulate extreme volatility or liquidity droughts. Second, real-time monitoring is essential—not simply of trades executed, but of the algorithm's internal state, decision pathways, and adherence to risk parameters. Third, there must be clearly defined kill switches and escalation protocols, ensuring that human operators can intervene decisively when anomalies occur. The irony is that some of the most robust algorithmic strategies succeed not because they operate without human input, but because they integrate human oversight as a non-negotiable safeguard.

Yet even with these safeguards, algorithms are still constrained by the limits of their creators' imagination. They are bounded systems, incapable of interpreting factors that lie outside their programmed scope. Political events, regulatory shifts, natural disasters, and technological breakthroughs can all trigger market reactions that defy statistical precedent. The unexpected removal of the Swiss franc's peg to the euro in January 2015 is one such example: within minutes of the announcement, currency markets convulsed, and automated systems built on assumptions of stability in the CHF/EUR pair suffered sharp losses. Many of these systems had never encountered a comparable event in their training data, leaving them effectively blind to its implications.

There is also the danger of correlated failure. As more traders adopt similar algorithmic strategies—often based on the same data sources, technical indicators, or machine learning frameworks—the likelihood increases that they will react in unison to the same signals. This herding effect can magnify market moves and accelerate losses, especially in illiquid conditions. The very efficiency that algorithms bring to execution can, in such moments, work against stability. Speed is a double-edged sword: it allows you to exit a position faster than most, but it also ensures that if you and thousands of others receive the same signal, the market impact is immediate and severe.

None of this diminishes the legitimate advantages that algorithms offer: the capacity to process vast amounts of data, execute with precision, and operate without the cognitive biases that impair human judgment. But *these strengths are conditional*. They depend on correct assumptions, high-quality data, and disciplined risk management. The moment any of these foundations falter, the algorithm's consistency becomes a liability rather than an asset. The belief in a "magic bullet" is dangerous precisely because it discourages ongoing scrutiny. It tempts traders to think of algorithms as self-correcting or adaptive in ways they are not. Without deliberate design, they do not learn from mistakes—they simply repeat them at scale.

The most effective algorithmic traders understand this asymmetry. They treat their systems not as black boxes to be revered, but as tools to be interrogated and refined continuously. They recognise that an algorithm's past performance is not a guarantee of future resilience, and that adaptability lies not in the code itself, but in the human capacity to re-evaluate and recalibrate it. An algorithm, however advanced, is still a model of the world, not the world itself. It is a map, and like any map, it is an abstraction—accurate enough to guide you when conditions align, but incomplete in ways that matter most when the terrain shifts unexpectedly.

To approach the market with the belief that an algorithm alone will deliver unbroken success is to misunderstand both the market and the machine. The market is a living, adaptive system shaped by countless interacting forces, many of them beyond quantification. The machine is a fixed set of instructions, however complex, operating within the boundaries of its design. The edge lies not in abandoning one for the other, but in knowing exactly where the strengths of the algorithm end and where the irreplaceable role of human judgment begins.

## The Bias Blind Spot

One of the most persistent misconceptions in trading is that the adoption of algorithms automatically strips human error out of the process. The thinking goes like this: if human judgment is prone to bias, and algorithms follow rules without emotion, then handing decision-making to machines should eliminate those psychological pitfalls. The reality is far less comforting. Algorithms do not erase bias—they often inherit it, absorb it, and in some cases, magnify it. The difference is that when bias is embedded in code, it becomes less visible and more difficult to challenge.

Bias begins with design. Every algorithm starts as an idea in someone's mind, and that idea is shaped by the designer's worldview, past experiences, and expectations about how markets work. Choices about which variables to include, which historical periods to analyse, and which risk tolerances to set are all expressions of subjective judgment. A trader who believes that small-cap stocks consistently outperform may, consciously or unconsciously, feed more small-cap data into their training set. A developer wary of high volatility may build algorithms that filter out aggressive opportunities, not because data supports it unequivocally, but because their personal risk aversion guides the logic. The code may execute without hesitation, but the parameters it follows are already steeped in human preference.

Even in purely data-driven strategies, bias can creep in through selection effects. Historical datasets are not neutral; they reflect the conditions, policies, and structural quirks of the periods they cover. A model trained exclusively on data from a decade-long bull market will internalise patterns of rising prices and muted drawdowns, leading to a dangerous overconfidence in similar conditions persisting. This was evident in the years before the 2008 financial crisis, when risk models in banks consistently underestimated the possibility of widespread mortgage defaults—not because the mathematics was faulty, but because the data it was built on came from an unusually stable housing market. The absence of a certain event in the training data does not mean it cannot happen; it simply means the algorithm has no reference point for recognising it.

There is also the problem of confirmation bias during backtesting. Traders are often tempted to adjust their models until the historical results look impressive—a process that, intentionally or not, "fits" the algorithm to the idiosyncrasies of the past. Each adjustment might be justified as fine-tuning, but in aggregate, it creates a system optimised for what has already happened, not for what will happen next. Once deployed in live markets, such strategies can unravel quickly when they encounter conditions outside their over-tailored comfort zone. The danger here is compounded by the seductive clarity of backtest charts, which present a clean, upward-sloping equity curve as evidence of robustness, masking the fact that this smoothness is often an artefact of hindsight rather than a product of predictive power.

Operational bias adds another layer of risk. Even if an algorithm is built on sound principles, the way it is monitored and adjusted can introduce distortions. Traders may be inclined to override a system after a string of losses, even when those losses fall within the statistical expectations of the strategy. Alternatively, they may increase position sizes after a streak of wins, convinced that the system has "found its groove." In both cases, emotional responses to short-term performance interfere with the long-term logic the algorithm was designed to follow. The irony is that while algorithms are touted as emotionless, their human operators often reintroduce the very impulses they were meant to avoid.

Bias is not only about fear and greed; it also manifests in the blind spots we fail to see. A developer might assume that their algorithm's risk controls are adequate because it passed a historical stress test. But stress tests are themselves constructed scenarios, defined by human imagination. If the test fails to include a scenario resembling a sudden regulatory ban, a flash liquidity freeze, or a cyberattack on market infrastructure, the algorithm may be entirely unprepared. This form of *availability bias*—overweighting scenarios we can readily imagine—means that models are often ill-equipped for events that have not yet entered the collective consciousness of market participants.

The rise of machine learning has introduced a new layer of subtlety to this problem. In theory, models that "learn" from data should adapt more effectively than static rule-based systems. In practice, they remain vulnerable to biases in their training inputs and in the labelling of data. If a classification model is trained to identify "profitable" trades based on past performance without accounting for transaction costs or market impact, it may systematically favour strategies that look good on paper but are infeasible in reality. Worse still, the opacity of complex models can make it difficult to identify where these biases are operating. Unlike a simple moving-average crossover strategy, whose logic can be explained in a sentence, a deep learning model with millions of parameters resists intuitive scrutiny. This opacity can lull traders into overconfidence, assuming that complexity equates to accuracy.

Recognising the bias blind spot requires both intellectual humility and methodological discipline. The first step is to accept that no model is free from human influence, however objective it appears. This acceptance shifts the goal from eliminating bias to identifying and mitigating it. That may mean using out-of-sample testing to check for overfitting, applying walk-forward optimisation rather than a single historical backtest, or deliberately introducing stress scenarios that challenge the model's assumptions. It also means documenting design choices and the rationale behind them, so that future reviews can trace the lineage of the algorithm's logic and identify where subjective decisions may have crept in.

Equally important is building a culture of challenge. Algorithms perform best when their outputs are treated as inputs to a decision process, not as final verdicts. This requires traders and risk managers to question why a system is making certain recommendations, to compare those recommendations against independent indicators, and to track the outcomes of decisions made with and without algorithmic influence. Such comparative analysis can highlight patterns in which the algorithm's guidance systematically underperforms, suggesting areas where bias may be distorting its logic.

Perhaps the most valuable insight is that bias in algorithms is not solely a technical problem—it is a behavioural one. The same cognitive shortcuts that lead a manual trader to misjudge risk or overvalue recent information can influence the design, deployment, and interpretation of automated systems. By acknowledging this, investors can resist the temptation to treat algorithms as neutral arbiters and instead approach them as collaborators—powerful, but fallible, partners in the pursuit of better decisions. An algorithm may not feel the pull of bias, but it can still carry it, invisibly, through every line of code it executes. The responsibility to spot and correct those distortions lies not with the machine, but with the human who built it, operates it, and depends on its judgment.

## Trust, but Verify

The most dangerous thing you can give an algorithm is your unquestioning faith. Blind trust turns a precision instrument into a liability because it removes the very safeguard that makes technology truly valuable: the human capacity for critical evaluation. In finance especially, where even small errors can cascade into catastrophic losses, the distinction between a trusted assistant and an unquestioned oracle is the line between disciplined strategy and reckless abdication of responsibility. Algorithms excel at processing speed, consistency, and scale, but they are not infallible interpreters of reality. They cannot intuit when market dynamics have shifted, nor can they recognise that the logic guiding them is no longer valid. They will keep executing the rules they've been given with tireless obedience, whether those rules are generating profits or quietly eroding your capital.

A mental model worth adopting is to view algorithms as highly competent analysts—capable of generating insights faster and with more detail than you could manage alone—but not as decision-makers in their own right. They can scan the market for patterns, calculate risk metrics, and flag anomalies without fatigue or bias of mood. Yet like any analyst, they can be wrong. Their perspective is shaped entirely by the data they are fed and the instructions they are given. The Knight Capital incident in 2012, in which a technical error caused hundreds of millions in losses within minutes, illustrates this vividly: the algorithm didn't "malfunction" in a conscious sense; it followed its code perfectly. What failed was the absence of a supervisory layer ready to question its behaviour in real time.

The philosophy of "trust, but verify" demands a balance of confidence and scepticism. Confidence is necessary because without it, you are likely to override algorithms prematurely or hesitate in letting them execute their strategies—undermining their very advantage. Scepticism is necessary because markets evolve, models degrade, and the accuracy of a system today does not guarantee its accuracy tomorrow. Verification in this context is not a one-off validation during the development phase; it is an ongoing discipline. It means monitoring live trades against expectations, reviewing performance in different market conditions, and checking whether the assumptions built into the system still hold true.

Verification also involves interrogating the source and quality of the data your algorithm uses. A strategy trained on incomplete or biased historical data will produce signals that carry those biases forward. If the dataset is skewed towards certain market phases or asset classes, the algorithm's recommendations will reflect that skew. The danger is compounded by the veneer of precision: statistical outputs and model-driven forecasts can appear authoritative even when the underlying inputs are flawed. A human operator applying "trust, but verify" will not take the outputs at face value, but will ask: *what is this system seeing, and what is it blind to?*

An important distinction emerges here between reactive and proactive verification. Reactive verification occurs when you investigate after something has gone wrong—when an algorithm has deviated from expectations or suffered a performance drop. Proactive verification means testing for weaknesses before the market exposes them. This can include running walk-forward tests, using out-of-sample data, applying Monte Carlo simulations to model random variations, and deliberately introducing stress conditions to see how the system behaves under extreme volatility or illiquidity. The goal is to surface fragility in controlled conditions, not in the heat of live trading.

This approach is not just about safeguarding against errors; it is about deepening your understanding of the system you are using. When you verify an algorithm's behaviour, you learn its strengths and its limits—when it thrives, when it struggles, and when it needs human intervention. Without this insight, you risk either overestimating its competence or underestimating its utility. Overestimation leads to dangerous passivity; underestimation leads to needless interference. Both diminish performance.

The tendency to see algorithms as oracles is partly psychological. They speak in numbers, charts, and backtested results—forms of output that convey an illusion of objectivity. This effect is magnified when the internal workings of the algorithm are complex or opaque, as with certain machine learning models. Faced with a "black box" whose internal logic is difficult to explain, some traders defer to its output simply because they cannot easily challenge it. The trust, but verify mindset counters this by treating opacity as a reason for *more* scrutiny, not less. If you cannot fully explain why the algorithm is making a given recommendation, you should be more, not less, cautious in acting on it.

Interestingly, the most successful institutional traders rarely operate on blind automation. Even in high-frequency environments, where trades are executed in microseconds, there are systems to monitor systems—meta-algorithms that detect unusual activity, human risk managers ready to intervene, and layers of redundancy designed to catch faults before they spiral. The lesson for the retail investor is clear: scale does not remove the need for oversight; if anything, it amplifies it. The more trades your system executes and the faster it does so, the more vigilant you must be about verifying that it is doing what it should.

Verification also extends beyond technical performance to strategic alignment. Markets change, and so should your algorithms. A model built for a low-interest-rate environment may need significant recalibration when rates rise sharply. An algorithm tuned to capitalise on trending markets may underperform in choppy, range-bound conditions. If you treat the algorithm as an oracle, you risk assuming that it will "figure out" the new environment on its own. If you treat it as an assistant, you recognise that it will need updated instructions, revised inputs, or even temporary suspension while you rethink its role.

Ultimately, "trust, but verify" is less about mistrusting technology and more about elevating the role of human judgment. It acknowledges that while algorithms can execute with a level of consistency and speed we cannot match, they cannot step outside themselves to question their own relevance. That responsibility rests with you. Trust allows you to benefit from their strengths; verification ensures those strengths remain aligned with your objectives. It is a partnership model—one in which the human provides strategic oversight and adaptability, and the machine delivers precision and discipline.

By approaching algorithms with this mindset, you avoid both extremes: the complacency of over-reliance and the inefficiency of constant interference. You preserve the advantages of automation without surrendering control. And perhaps most importantly, you remain the ultimate decision-maker in your own trading—delegating execution, but never delegating responsibility. In markets where conditions shift, surprises emerge, and yesterday's certainty can become today's liability, that balance is not just prudent; it is essential.

# Chapter 2
# Seeing the Market Differently

Markets do not communicate in words; they speak in movements. Prices ascend and descend, volumes swell and recede, volatility surges and diminishes—an intricate choreography of overlapping motions. Historically, decoding these signals relied almost entirely on human vigilance. Traders honed the craft of reading the tape, memorising seasonal rhythms, or reacting instinctively to shifts in order flow. The most adept could discern subtle changes in market "tone" that eluded their colleagues. Yet even the sharpest human eye has its limits: our capacity to process information is finite, we tire, and we often overlook anomalies that defy expectation. Algorithms, in contrast, traverse millions of data points without fatigue, uncover patterns that escape intuition, and observe multiple markets at once. In essence, they perceive dimensions of the market that we cannot—and in doing so, they redefine what it means to be truly informed.

Take, for instance, the challenge of identifying correlations. A human analyst might notice that a particular sector tends to rally when oil prices decline, or that a currency strengthens following specific central bank announcements. But what if the correlation spans dozens of variables—oil, shipping indices, credit spreads, weather events, corporate earnings revisions—interacting across different timeframes? Such a pattern could lie hidden in plain sight within publicly available data, yet remain invisible without computational intervention. Algorithms built to detect multi-dimensional relationships can reveal these insights in minutes. It is not magic; it is meticulousness and endurance. The advantage lies in their ability to hold the entire puzzle in view rather than piecing it together fragment by fragment.

Equally, algorithms surpass humans in distinguishing signal from noise. Modern markets generate a torrent of information: every price tick, every posted order, each news headline, social media mention, or shift in implied volatility. For the discretionary trader, this flood can be paralysing. We tend to overreact to recent or dramatic events, weighting them disproportionately in our decisions. This cognitive bias—the recency effect—turns ephemeral noise into seemingly meaningful trends. Properly designed algorithms apply filters, assessing the statistical significance of events within their historical context. Thousands of inconsequential fluctuations are ignored, leaving only movements that surpass predefined thresholds for predictive value. The outcome is clarity: traders operate on a narrower, more meaningful dataset, rather than drowning in a sea of trivia.

Many assume speed is the ultimate edge. Certainly, in domains like high-frequency trading, milliseconds matter—firms exploit fleeting opportunities that vanish in microseconds. But for most market participants, the difference between one-second and one-minute execution is trivial. Indeed, obsession with haste can backfire. Behavioural finance shows that impatience often undermines returns; investors habitually sell winners too early and cling to losers too long, driven by the discomfort of uncertainty. Algorithms instil discipline not by accelerating decisions indiscriminately, but by identifying when patience is statistically advantageous. A breakout signal may gain reliability only after hours of confirmation, or volatility spikes may yield better returns once the initial surge subsides. Here, measured delay—not rapidity—becomes the strategic advantage, and algorithms can determine precisely when that is the case.

Underlying all this is a profound shift: data is now the preeminent currency. Not insider tips, not whispered rumours, but structured, timely, and clean data—and the skill to interpret it. In a market where most participants have identical price feeds, access alone confers little advantage; the differentiator is turning raw data into actionable insight before others do. This is why trading firms invest heavily in alternative data: satellite imagery to gauge retail footfall, cargo logs to anticipate commodity movements, web scraping to track product pricing. The sophistication of the sources matters less than the discipline in interpreting them. Algorithms can process terabytes of such information, testing countless hypotheses simultaneously, while human teams would require weeks merely to reach a preliminary conclusion.

To perceive the market differently is not to supplant human judgment with machine vision but to broaden what can be apprehended and understood. Humans excel at synthesising narratives from disparate facts, appreciating the qualitative context of events—a sudden policy change, an unexpected geopolitical flare-up, or shifts in consumer sentiment. Algorithms, on the other hand, parse immense volumes of quantitative data without fatigue or bias. The true edge arises when these capabilities are combined: the algorithm uncovers patterns invisible to the naked eye, and the human evaluates their real-world significance. This partnership transforms market navigation—not by rendering the trader omniscient, but by making them better informed, more disciplined, and less vulnerable to noise and impatience.

In the chapters that follow, we will move beyond the notion that market acumen is purely a matter of instinct or intuition. The contemporary advantage lies in the fusion of human insight with machine precision—a transformation not in what we see, but in how we are able to see it.

## Patterns Beyond Human Perception

Financial markets are not random in the pure mathematical sense, yet the patterns they produce often defy the limits of unaided human perception. What looks like noise to the naked eye can conceal structures, relationships, and sequences of cause and effect that only become visible when examined with computational precision. The human brain excels at spotting simple, repeating forms—a trend line, a price cycle, a seasonal rhythm—but once the complexity rises beyond a few variables, we quickly reach a cognitive ceiling. Algorithms, on the other hand, are unburdened by this limit. They can hold thousands of variables in active comparison, assess correlations across decades of historical data, and flag anomalies that occur in fleeting, non-linear bursts—patterns so subtle that no trader, however skilled, could detect them in real time.

One of the clearest demonstrations of this advantage comes from cross-asset correlation analysis. Imagine trying to assess whether a change in copper prices influences the movement of a mid-cap technology stock. A human might glance at charts of both and draw some tentative conclusions, but the task becomes impossible when expanded to thousands of potential relationships: commodities, currencies, indices, interest rates, sentiment indicators, and weather data. Algorithms can calculate correlation coefficients across these vast datasets in milliseconds, identify when they are statistically significant, and detect shifts in correlation strength over time. What emerges is not a vague hunch but a mathematically robust map of interconnections—maps that often reveal surprising drivers of price action, such as the influence of freight shipping rates on retail stock performance, or the predictive power of certain credit spreads for equity volatility.

Beyond correlation, algorithms excel at anomaly detection—identifying events that deviate from expected patterns in ways too small or too brief for humans to catch.

A large institutional trader might place an order in such a way that it subtly changes the shape of the order book for a few seconds; a human scanning a screen would miss it, but an algorithm trained to model normal market microstructure would flag it instantly. In risk management, this ability is equally powerful. An algorithm might detect that a normally tight correlation between two assets has suddenly and sharply weakened, suggesting an underlying market stress that has not yet shown up in price indices. This kind of early warning is difficult to replicate without computational assistance, as it requires continuous, high-frequency monitoring of relationships across multiple dimensions.

The superiority of algorithms in perceiving complex patterns is not just about speed; it is about scope and depth. Humans are linear thinkers by default, often focusing on one or two explanatory variables and projecting them forward. Markets, however, are multi-causal systems, where outcomes emerge from the interaction of countless inputs. Machine learning models, particularly those using techniques like random forests or gradient boosting, can rank the importance of different variables in predicting an outcome—allowing traders to see that a factor they previously ignored, such as regional electricity demand, carries far more predictive weight than a factor they assumed was primary. This is not intuition replacing data; it is data expanding intuition.

A practical example is the detection of regime shifts—points at which the statistical properties of a market change so that past models no longer apply. For a discretionary trader, these shifts often reveal themselves only after sustained losses or missed opportunities. Algorithms, by contrast, can monitor volatility clustering, distribution skewness, and other statistical markers in real time, signalling when a strategy calibrated for one environment is entering another. This is not a matter of "knowing the future," but of seeing the early signs of change quickly enough to adjust. The advantage is not merely academic; it can be the difference between exiting a position before a drawdown and holding it until the loss becomes unrecoverable.

Importantly, the patterns algorithms reveal are not always intuitive, and that is precisely why they are valuable. In the years leading up to the 2008 financial crisis, some credit derivatives began showing pricing anomalies that hinted at rising systemic risk. The signs were there in the data, but because they did not fit the prevailing narrative, most human analysts overlooked them. Models designed to monitor such dislocations might have raised alarms earlier—provided that their operators were willing to act on what seemed, at the time, to be an improbable signal. Here lies one of the enduring tensions in algorithmic trading: the most actionable insights often arrive in forms that challenge human expectation, requiring the discipline to trust the validity of the method even when the message is uncomfortable.

It is worth noting that while algorithms can uncover patterns far beyond human reach, they are not immune to false positives. Complex statistical searches inevitably produce relationships that occur by chance rather than causal connection—what statisticians call spurious correlations. Without careful validation, a model might "discover" that equity markets rise when a particular sports team wins, or when a certain phrase trends online, purely because the two happened to align in the historical record. This is where the partnership between human judgment and machine detection becomes critical. The machine can surface candidates for further investigation, but the human must assess whether those candidates are plausible and grounded in an underlying economic or behavioural mechanism.

The expansion of data sources in recent years has magnified this capability. Algorithms now ingest not only traditional price and volume data but also satellite imagery, shipping manifests, transaction-level credit card data, and sentiment extracted from news and social media. Each of these streams contains patterns invisible to human observation simply because of their volume and complexity. A trader could not realistically read millions of tweets or process every global cargo departure in real time, but an algorithm can summarise this activity into actionable metrics, flagging sentiment shifts or supply chain bottlenecks that might influence asset prices before the mainstream financial press takes notice.

What emerges from all this is a reframing of what it means to "see" the market. Human traders still hold an advantage in interpreting patterns within a broader qualitative context, but algorithms extend the field of vision into territories we could never reach unaided. They can scan the entire chessboard while we focus on the immediate square in front of us. This does not render human skill obsolete; rather, it challenges us to think more deeply about where our interpretive strengths lie and how best to deploy them once the machine has done the heavy lifting of detection. The goal is not to surrender judgment to an algorithm, but to let its perception stretch our own—so that the patterns we act upon are not only visible, but also truly meaningful.

## Signal vs. Noise

The modern trader faces a paradox that would have baffled their predecessors: the problem is no longer finding information, but filtering it. Markets now produce a continuous torrent of data, both structured and unstructured. Every price change, every order placed or cancelled, every headline, corporate filing, analyst note, social media post, shipping record, and consumer transaction feeds into a vast and chaotic information ecosystem. The human mind, evolved for survival in environments with limited stimuli, is ill-equipped to separate the valuable few signals from the overwhelming volume of noise. Algorithms, when designed with precision, excel at this task—not by consuming more data than humans, but by applying disciplined, rule-based criteria to decide what merits attention and what should be discarded.

The distinction between signal and noise in financial markets is not always obvious. Price fluctuations, for example, contain both—the signal might be the beginning of a sustained trend, while the noise is the random oscillation around it. Without tools to filter them, traders are prone to seeing patterns where none exist, a bias known as apophenia. A stock might tick higher three days in a row, prompting a human observer to believe momentum is building, when in reality the moves are statistically insignificant against the background volatility. An algorithm can quantify this significance in real time, comparing the movement to historical norms and volatility-adjusted expectations, thereby reducing the risk of acting on false patterns.

Noise is not limited to market ticks. News and commentary contribute their own distortions. Financial media thrives on immediacy and drama, often elevating minor developments to headline status and assigning causality to events that are, in truth, just market noise. Social media amplifies this effect, creating viral narratives that can move prices in the short term but rarely reflect deeper fundamentals. Algorithms trained to process natural language can ingest these streams, measure sentiment trends, and filter out repetitive or low-impact content, allowing traders to focus only on developments that historically correlate with measurable market impact. This capability is particularly valuable in avoiding the trap of overreacting to isolated anecdotes or the loudest voices in the room.

The sheer scale of modern data streams demands this kind of filtering. In equities alone, high-frequency trading generates millions of order book updates per second. Add to that the global bond, currency, and commodity markets, each with its own data feed, and the challenge becomes evident: without an automated filtering process, the signal is buried. Algorithms can be configured to monitor multiple asset classes simultaneously, flagging only those anomalies that cross a predefined threshold of statistical or economic significance. This reduces the cognitive load on human operators, who can then devote their attention to interpreting fewer, but higher-quality, alerts.

A well-designed filtering process is not static. What counts as noise in one market regime may be signal in another. For instance, in a stable interest rate environment, small shifts in short-term bond yields might be inconsequential. In a period of central bank uncertainty, those same shifts could precede major currency moves or sector rotations. Algorithms can adapt to these changing contexts by dynamically adjusting their filters, weighting inputs differently based on current volatility, liquidity conditions, and macroeconomic drivers. This adaptability is what gives them an edge over rigid, rule-bound human routines.

Yet the ability to filter is not just about excluding irrelevant data; it is also about recognising the incompleteness of the signals that remain. Algorithms can quantify the confidence level of each signal, indicating whether it is based on a robust statistical pattern or on a weaker, more ambiguous correlation. This transparency allows traders to calibrate their responses—perhaps acting more decisively on high-confidence signals while monitoring low-confidence ones for confirmation. Without such gradation, the risk is binary thinking: either overreacting to marginal signals or ignoring them altogether.

The famous hedge fund manager Ray Dalio once remarked that "the greatest mistake investors make is to believe that what happened in the recent past will continue." This bias is a direct consequence of failing to distinguish signal from noise. Algorithms counteract it by embedding longer historical baselines into their analysis. A one-week rally in a sector might look compelling in isolation, but when placed in the context of a ten-year cycle, it may register as entirely ordinary. By maintaining these broader perspectives in memory, algorithms help prevent traders from being seduced by recency.

However, there is a trap here as well: filtering can become over-filtering. If thresholds are set too high, genuine early signals may be dismissed as noise. This is where the human element is essential. An experienced trader can recognise when an algorithm's conservatism is causing it to miss opportunities—perhaps because the signal in question aligns with qualitative factors the algorithm does not process, such as a shift in political sentiment or an emerging technology trend. The most effective workflows build in a feedback loop where human operators can flag missed signals for re-evaluation, gradually refining the system's filters without loosening them indiscriminately.

One of the clearest demonstrations of algorithmic filtering power comes from the world of statistical arbitrage. Here, algorithms track pairs or baskets of related securities, identifying temporary divergences in their price relationships. The majority of such divergences are noise—momentary mismatches caused by liquidity imbalances or order execution timing. But a small fraction represent genuine mispricings with a high probability of reverting. The challenge is to detect these outliers in real time without being distracted by the thousands of false positives. By setting precise thresholds based on standard deviations from historical means, and by filtering according to market conditions, algorithms can pinpoint the true opportunities and discard the rest.

The strategic advantage of filtering is cumulative. A single noisy trade avoided might not seem transformative, but avoiding dozens over the course of a year preserves capital, reduces transaction costs, and prevents strategy drift. More importantly, by freeing the trader from the constant bombardment of low-value stimuli, it sharpens focus on the decisions that truly matter. The aim is not to process *more* information than competitors, but to process *less*, of higher quality, and to act on it faster and with greater conviction.

In this way, algorithms shift the role of the human trader from that of an overburdened information processor to that of a decision architect—someone who defines what counts as signal, sets the parameters for its detection, and then applies judgement to the filtered outputs. This reallocation of cognitive resources is what makes the filtering process so powerful. The machine excels at sifting the infinite; the human excels at deciding what to do with what remains. In the noise-saturated environment of modern markets, mastering this division of labour is not merely an efficiency gain—it is the foundation of a sustainable edge.

## Why Speed Matters—But Not Always

In the popular imagination, speed in trading is synonymous with advantage. The image of a lightning-fast algorithm executing thousands of trades in fractions of a second has become shorthand for market dominance, reinforced by headlines about high-frequency trading firms exploiting microsecond leads to generate outsized profits. There is truth to this association—speed can confer an unassailable edge in certain contexts—but it is also incomplete. In many situations, rapid execution offers no meaningful benefit, and in some cases it actively undermines performance. The more mature view is that *speed is a tool, not a virtue in itself*; it is valuable only when applied to circumstances where time truly determines outcome.

The clearest example of speed as a decisive advantage is in the microstructure of modern markets. When multiple participants compete for the same liquidity, a fraction-of-a-second delay can mean the difference between filling an order at the desired price and missing it entirely. This is the domain of high-frequency trading (HFT), where firms invest millions in microwave transmission networks, co-located servers, and optimised code to shave microseconds from round-trip execution times. For strategies exploiting fleeting arbitrage—such as detecting price discrepancies between related securities and executing simultaneous trades to lock in the spread—being first is everything. The opportunity evaporates the moment the market adjusts, making speed not just important, but existential to the strategy's viability.

Yet outside such narrow windows, the advantage of raw execution speed diminishes sharply. Many trading strategies operate on timeframes where market conditions do not change meaningfully within seconds—or even minutes. For a position trader adjusting exposure based on macroeconomic trends or corporate fundamentals, the difference between executing at 10:02:15 and 10:02:45 is negligible. In fact, an obsession with immediacy can encourage overtrading, reacting to every tick as if it were significant, and eroding returns through transaction costs and unnecessary churn. Behavioural finance research consistently shows that overreaction to short-term price movements is a key driver of underperformance, especially among retail traders. Algorithms that enforce patience—by executing only when certain statistical or structural conditions are met—often outperform those that respond to every fluctuation.

Patience has another, less obvious advantage: it can allow a trade to mature into a more favourable setup. Consider breakout trading. A hasty execution at the first hint of a breakout often results in being caught in a false move, as short-term volatility tests and retests the breakout level before a genuine trend emerges. An algorithm tuned to wait for confirmation—perhaps requiring a breakout to hold beyond a set number of bars or to be accompanied by an increase in volume—will enter later than the fastest possible execution, but with a higher probability of success. This approach recognises that speed without selectivity is just early participation in a coin toss.

The tension between speed and patience is not purely technical; it is deeply behavioural. Humans tend to equate fast action with competence, a bias that behavioural psychologists link to our evolutionary history. In environments where immediate response to threats was essential for survival, hesitation could be fatal. Markets exploit this wiring. Price movements, especially sharp ones, create a sense of urgency that triggers fear of missing out (FOMO) or fear of loss. Traders rush to act, often without fully processing whether the move is meaningful or sustainable. Algorithms, insulated from this emotional trigger, can enforce rules that delay execution until criteria are met, effectively protecting the trader from their own impulses.

Speed can also mislead in environments where liquidity is deceptive. In thinly traded assets, executing too quickly can signal intentions to the market, prompting adverse movement before the order is fully filled—a phenomenon known as market impact. In such cases, algorithms designed for stealth rather than raw velocity can achieve better outcomes by slicing orders into smaller parts and executing them gradually, blending into the normal flow of trading activity. Here, slowness is not hesitation but a deliberate tactic to preserve price.

One of the more subtle cases where speed can be detrimental is during information releases. Major economic announcements or corporate earnings reports often cause immediate price spikes as participants digest the news. High-speed execution in the first moments may capture an initial move, but it also exposes the trader to heightened volatility and whipsaw reversals as the market overreacts, reassesses, and settles into a more rational pricing. Algorithms programmed to wait for a set period after a news event—allowing initial emotional reactions to burn off—can avoid being whipsawed and enter trades with greater clarity on market direction.

This interplay of speed and patience can be framed as a question of signal maturity. In some strategies, the signal is fleeting and must be acted on instantly to have value. In others, the signal gains reliability as it develops over time, making immediate execution not just unnecessary but counterproductive. The challenge lies in designing systems that recognise which category a given situation belongs to, and that adjust behaviour accordingly. This is where adaptive algorithms—those that incorporate both market state detection and execution logic—outperform rigidly fast or slow systems.

The behavioural finance literature reinforces the value of this adaptability. Studies have shown that traders who can resist the urge to respond instantly to price changes tend to make more deliberate, higher-quality decisions. Algorithms can be built to enforce this discipline, but the human operator must still decide when speed is justified and when restraint is wiser. Blindly pursuing one over the other turns a nuanced tool into a blunt instrument.

Seen in this light, the most effective use of speed is strategic rather than constant. It is about identifying the rare contexts where time truly is money and concentrating execution resources there, while allowing patience to govern in all other circumstances. This requires rejecting the cultural myth that faster is always better—a myth that persists largely because the most visible stories in financial media involve high-speed successes, not the quieter, steadier gains of well-timed patience.

Ultimately, speed is an amplifier. In the right context, it magnifies advantage; in the wrong one, it magnifies error. The skill lies in knowing when the window of opportunity is genuinely closing and when it is merely perceived to be closing under the pressure of noise and emotion. Algorithms can help make this distinction with consistency that human traders struggle to maintain. But as with all tools in trading, their effectiveness depends not on their inherent capabilities, but on the precision and wisdom with which they are deployed.

### Data as the New Edge

For most of the twentieth century, the archetype of a market edge was access to privileged information. The most coveted advantage was knowing something the market did not—an earnings result before it was released, an unannounced merger, a change in policy whispered over dinner with the right politician. Regulation and enforcement were far from perfect, but the idea was consistent: the trader with the best "inside tip" held the winning card. In modern markets, that model is increasingly obsolete. Insider information has not disappeared, but the legal and reputational risks of using it have multiplied, enforcement has tightened, and more importantly, the sheer volume and velocity of public data has eroded the notion that secrecy is the only path to advantage. Today, *the most sustainable edge lies not in possession of secret facts, but in the ability to extract meaning from vast, complex, and often chaotic data before others can.*

The shift is partly a function of technology. Market data feeds now stream prices, volumes, order book depth, and derivatives pricing in real time. Beyond the exchanges, countless alternative data sources—satellite imagery, shipping manifests, transaction-level credit card data, weather patterns, corporate website traffic—are available to those who know where to look. This abundance has inverted the problem. Where once the challenge was acquiring information, the challenge now is filtering, structuring, and interpreting it in a way that yields timely, actionable insight. In this environment, data itself is not rare; *understanding* is.

Consider the case of retail foot traffic data derived from anonymised mobile phone location signals. This is not privileged information; it is collected legally from consenting users, aggregated by third parties, and sold as a product. Analysts who can link this data to revenue estimates may predict a retailer's quarterly performance weeks before the official results. The signal is hidden in plain sight, and it does not require breaking any rules—only the technical skill to clean, analyse, and contextualise the numbers. The firm that can do this consistently gains a repeatable advantage over competitors who either lack the data or cannot process it quickly enough to act.

Data-driven advantage is not confined to fundamental forecasting. In market microstructure, algorithms ingest the constant churn of bids, offers, and executions to detect patterns invisible to the naked eye. A surge in hidden liquidity at a particular price level, the sudden withdrawal of limit orders in a correlated asset, or a consistent time-of-day drift in spreads may all carry exploitable meaning. These are not tips from an insider; they are patterns discernible only through continuous measurement, statistical modelling, and interpretation. The same applies to volatility forecasting, where historical price data, options market activity, and even cross-asset signals can be combined to produce probabilistic scenarios more accurate than intuition or news headlines.

The competitive nature of markets means that raw data, once valuable, decays quickly as more participants gain access to it. The differentiator becomes the *processing pipeline*: how quickly and effectively you can convert raw inputs into decisions. This involves not only algorithms that automate analysis but also the infrastructure to acquire and store data efficiently, the statistical frameworks to avoid false correlations, and the human judgment to decide when to act. A dataset on its own has no intrinsic value; it gains value only when it is part of a coherent process that turns it into insight and action.

It is tempting to think that more data always means better insight, but this is not necessarily true. Without careful curation, more data can mean more noise, and without robust analytical frameworks, it can create an illusion of understanding. The proliferation of data can also lead to *confirmation bias*, where analysts search for patterns that reinforce their pre-existing beliefs, overlooking contradictory evidence buried in the dataset. This is why the most successful data-driven strategies combine algorithmic detection with strict out-of-sample testing, validation across independent datasets, and a willingness to abandon patterns that do not hold up under scrutiny.

The growing importance of data access and interpretation has also reshaped the skill set required to compete. In earlier decades, a trader's edge might have come from interpersonal networks, deep sector knowledge, or sheer trading floor experience. Those traits still matter, but they are no longer sufficient on their own. Today's competitive advantage often hinges on fluency in statistical reasoning, familiarity with programming and database tools, and an understanding of how to integrate disparate data sources into a single decision-making process. The best discretionary traders increasingly work in symbiosis with data scientists and technologists, blurring the lines between traditional trading and quantitative research.

This transformation is visible in the rise of *alternative data funds*—investment firms built around sourcing and exploiting non-traditional datasets. These funds invest heavily not only in acquiring data but in developing proprietary models to extract meaning from it. Their returns come not from knowing a secret that no one else could theoretically obtain, but from *acting faster and with greater conviction on publicly or commercially available information*. In this model, speed of insight is as important as speed of execution; the first firm to interpret a relevant signal and act on it holds the edge, even if competitors gain access to the same raw data minutes later.

The philosophical shift here is profound. In the old paradigm, information advantage was binary—you either had the tip or you didn't. In the data-driven paradigm, advantage is continuous and probabilistic. It is about constantly refining your models, testing your assumptions, and seeking marginal improvements in predictive power. A one per cent edge in forecasting accuracy, repeated consistently, compounds into a significant performance differential over time. This is why data-focused strategies are less about chasing a single big insight and more about building a disciplined, repeatable process for generating many small ones.

It is also worth recognising the democratizing potential of this shift. Insider tips by definition favour those with privileged access to closed networks. Data, while not free, is far more widely available. Retail traders, independent researchers, and small funds can now access many of the same datasets that large institutions use, often through subscription services or public APIs. The barrier to entry is no longer knowing the right person; it is knowing how to work with the information once you have it. This levels the playing field in theory, though in practice, the resources to process large datasets and the expertise to interpret them still confer an advantage to better-capitalised players.

Still, the arc of change is clear: *in modern markets, the primary bottleneck is not access to information but the ability to separate the meaningful from the irrelevant, the causal from the coincidental, and the timely from the outdated*. Mastery of data is mastery of perception. It determines not just what you see in the market, but how early and how accurately you see it—and in a competitive environment where marginal gains accumulate into durable advantages, that makes it the most valuable currency you can hold.

# Chapter 3
# Building Your Decision Engine

In markets characterised by ceaseless complexity and relentless noise, the act of making decisions is both the trader's sharpest instrument and their most frequent pitfall. Algorithms promise discipline, yet their strength is inseparable from the clarity of the principles and aims that guide them. Without a well-defined foundation, even the most advanced system risks collapse under ambiguity. A decision engine is far more than a tangle of formulas and code; it is the distilled embodiment of an investment philosophy, codified into rules that can be tested, replicated, and refined—untainted by mood swings, impulses, or distraction.

The first step is deceptively straightforward: knowing exactly what you intend to achieve. It sounds banal, yet in practice, most participants operate on aspirations rather than precise objectives. "I want to make money" or "I want to outperform the market" is too vague to translate into actionable code. Clear, algorithm-friendly targets resemble statements such as, "Achieve an average monthly return of 1% with a maximum drawdown of 5%," or, "Capture short-term momentum in the US equity market with positions held for under five days." These parameters give both machine and trader a concrete benchmark, enabling evaluation without recourse to subjective impressions. Ambiguity, in this context, is the algorithm's adversary.

Once objectives are established, they must be expressed through logical, conditional rules—the classic 'if-then' statements that constitute the architecture of algorithmic thought. Here, traders often err, equating more conditions and parameters with greater sophistication. In reality, the most effective rule-based systems frequently begin with startling simplicity. "If the price closes above the 50-day moving average, then buy; if below, sell" may appear rudimentary next to multi-factor models, yet it is clear, testable, and unambiguous. Its virtue lies in leaving minimal space for subjective interference. Human insight still shapes rule design and interpretation, but execution is mechanical—free from hesitation, second-guessing, and the cognitive clutter that afflicts human decision-making.

The temptation to fit these rules ever more tightly to historical data is potent. The backtest gleams; the strategy appears flawless. This is the lure of overfitting: crafting an algorithm perfect for the past, blind to the future. Overfitting is not a mere academic nuisance; it is the silent assassin of trading systems that, while appearing invincible on paper, crumble in live markets. Confusing coincidence with causality, mistaking noise for signal—these are the traps. Statistically, the model has captured quirks unlikely to repeat. Practically, it is akin to designing a lock for a key that no longer fits. Effective decision engines counter this through cross-validation, out-of-sample testing, and the ruthless elimination of variables that offer no demonstrable predictive value. The principle is simple: robustness trumps historical perfection.

Hence the potency of the Minimum Viable Algorithm. Just as start-ups deploy a minimum viable product to gauge market reaction, traders can begin with the simplest rules aligned with their objectives. A minimum viable algorithm pares away complexity, concentrating on the strategy's core logic. This approach confers two advantages: it clarifies which components genuinely drive performance, and it allows rapid iteration unencumbered by a sprawling codebase. Early trials prioritise stress-testing assumptions rather than maximising returns—observing outcomes when markets trend sharply, meander sideways, spike in volatility, or lose liquidity. Complexity is introduced later, but only when it demonstrably enhances real-world performance.

Constructing a decision engine, then, is an exercise in disciplined abstraction. Goals are defined, translated into unambiguous rules, shielded from over-optimisation, and initially framed as minimally viable structures. Iteration becomes measured expansion, each new element justified by evidence rather than aesthetics or the allure of sophistication. The final product is dynamic, evolving alongside markets, data sources, and the trader's comprehension. Yet its foundations—clarity of purpose, logical structure, resistance to overfitting, and incremental development—remain unwavering. In a realm where noise is relentless and tempo unceasing, such a framework is not merely advantageous; it is indispensable.

## Clarifying Your Investment Goals

Most investors think they have goals. Fewer have ones that mean anything to a machine. The difference is not semantic—it is structural. A human can operate for years on vague intentions such as "grow my capital" or "achieve financial independence," adjusting instinctively to changing circumstances. An algorithm has no such flexibility. It will not infer your meaning or improvise around your ambiguity; it will do exactly what you tell it, no more and no less. If the goal is not expressed in clear, measurable, and testable terms, the system is either doomed to operate blindly or, worse, to optimise for an outcome you did not intend. The first step in building any decision engine is therefore to convert abstract aspirations into precise targets that can be codified without guesswork.

Precision in goal-setting begins with recognising that markets are not friendly to imprecision. Consider two traders: one aims to "maximise returns," the other to "achieve an average monthly return of 1% with a maximum drawdown of 5% over a rolling 12-month period." The former goal is aspirational; the latter is operational. The second trader has embedded constraints (drawdown limits), time horizons (monthly, rolling 12 months), and performance metrics (percentage return) that can be evaluated objectively. This clarity allows for algorithmic translation. In code, such a target becomes a set of conditional triggers for entering and exiting trades, adjusting position sizes, or halting activity entirely when drawdowns breach a threshold. Vague goals, by contrast, cannot be coded without guesswork—and guesswork, when automated, produces chaos.

The discipline of algorithm-friendly goal setting forces a deeper confrontation with your actual priorities. Do you care more about absolute returns or about preserving capital? Is your appetite for volatility high or low? Would you accept prolonged periods of inactivity if it meant avoiding false signals, or do you prefer frequent trades with more noise in the outcomes? Each of these questions translates directly into parameters—maximum position sizes, stop-loss limits, signal thresholds—that an algorithm can act on without interpretation. The exercise is not just about feeding instructions to a machine; it is about making your own priorities explicit enough that you could hand them to a stranger and expect them to make consistent decisions on your behalf.

It is here that many investors discover a gap between what they think they want and what they are actually prepared to tolerate. Someone might declare they seek aggressive growth, but the first drawdown of 20% has them abandoning the strategy in panic. Others may claim to value capital preservation above all, yet they find themselves frustrated by the sluggish pace of low-volatility returns. *The process of clarifying goals is not merely technical; it is psychological.* An honest definition of objectives must account for your behavioural tendencies under stress, because algorithms do not operate in a vacuum—they operate in markets that will routinely test your limits. If your rules ignore your psychological reality, you will end up overriding them, defeating the very point of automation.

Historical examples show how costly unclear objectives can be. Hedge funds that deploy high-frequency strategies without strict risk caps may deliver spectacular gains in benign conditions, only to implode in periods of illiquidity because their algorithms had no embedded "kill switches." Conversely, some retail traders deploy conservative rule-sets intended to protect them from losses, only to find that their systems barely trade at all, producing negligible returns that fall short of their financial needs. In both cases, the failure lies in a mismatch between actual objectives and the parameters encoded into the system. The algorithm did exactly what it was told; the problem was in the telling.

Translating goals into algorithmic terms also involves decomposing them into measurable components. "Outperform the market" is not a measurable goal without defining the benchmark, the time horizon, and the metrics of comparison. Is "the market" the S&P 500? The MSCI World Index? Are you comparing total returns, risk-adjusted returns, or the Sharpe ratio? Without such precision, you cannot verify whether the algorithm is delivering on its mandate. More importantly, without measurable benchmarks, you cannot iterate effectively. An algorithm without a measurable goal is like a laboratory experiment without a hypothesis—there is nothing to test against, nothing to improve upon.

Yet clarity does not mean rigidity. The market environment shifts, and objectives must be re-evaluated in light of new realities. A strategy optimised for ultra-low interest rates may be unfit in a high-rate environment; a volatility-averse approach might miss opportunities in a sustained bull run. The point of algorithm-friendly objectives is not to lock you into a fixed path indefinitely, but to create a stable foundation from which changes can be made deliberately, based on evidence rather than impulse. The framework for your goals should therefore include *review intervals*, predefined moments when performance is evaluated against objectives, and parameters are adjusted if justified.

A useful mental model is to think of investment goals as the blueprint of a building and the algorithm as the construction crew. Without a detailed blueprint—measurements, materials, tolerances—the crew can only guess at your intentions, and their guesses may be expensive to correct. But even a perfect blueprint can become obsolete if the purpose of the building changes; you would not design a library the same way you would design a hospital. Clear goals provide direction, but they must be accompanied by a process for reassessment. This is not a flaw in the system; it is the mechanism by which the system stays relevant.

Finally, the discipline of clarifying investment goals has a filtering effect: it forces you to confront which ambitions are worth pursuing in the first place. The process exposes wishful thinking and forces trade-offs into the open. You cannot simultaneously maximise returns, minimise volatility, and maintain full liquidity at all times; something must give. By defining priorities with algorithmic precision, you are not just making your machine smarter—you are making yourself a more disciplined investor. In this sense, the act of clarifying goals is not a preparatory step before the "real" work of building an algorithm; it is the first substantive act of strategy itself. The strength of your decision engine will always rest on the strength of the objectives that drive it, and no amount of code can compensate for a foundation built on ambiguity.

## Rule-Based Thinking

At the core of every successful algorithm lies a simple yet profound principle: decisions must be made through explicit, testable rules, not vague impressions or reactive impulses. This is the logic of *if-then* thinking—if a defined condition is met, then a predetermined action follows. It is deceptively simple, yet it forces a level of clarity and discipline that few discretionary traders maintain consistently. For humans, ambiguity is tolerable and often inevitable; we can weigh a dozen competing factors, improvise around uncertainty, and sometimes rely on intuition. Machines have no such luxury. They require instructions that leave no room for interpretation.

The elegance of rule-based logic is in its ability to transform complex decision-making into a chain of binary evaluations. Consider a basic moving average crossover strategy: *If* the short-term moving average rises above the long-term moving average, *then* buy. *If* the short-term falls below the long-term, *then* sell. The algorithm does not "think" about whether the market feels overheated or undervalued; it executes the rule exactly as written. While this may appear simplistic, the strength lies in consistency. Human decision-making under pressure often suffers from bias, hesitation, or overconfidence. A well-designed rule-based system is immune to mood swings and narrative seduction—it acts identically on a quiet Tuesday morning as it does during a market-wide sell-off.

However, the simplicity of *if-then* logic can be misleading. Effective rules require precision in both their triggers and their responses. Vague conditions—"buy when the market looks strong"—cannot be translated into machine-readable code without reducing them to quantifiable indicators, such as price momentum exceeding a specific percentage over a defined period. The act of crafting such definitions forces the designer to confront the underlying rationale: why that percentage, why that timeframe, why that indicator? This intellectual discipline often exposes weaknesses in strategies that, when applied manually, might have felt intuitively sound.

Real-world algorithmic systems demonstrate the range of sophistication possible within a rule-based framework. At the simplest end, retail traders might employ fixed stop-loss and take-profit levels tied to entry prices. At the most complex, institutional funds run multi-layered conditionals where an initial signal triggers only if confirmed by secondary indicators, risk constraints, and broader market context. For example: *If* a momentum signal exceeds threshold X *and* volatility remains below threshold Y *and* portfolio exposure to the sector is less than Z%, *then* initiate a position of size N. Each additional condition reduces false positives but also risks missing legitimate opportunities. This is the trade-off inherent in rule construction: tighter rules improve accuracy at the cost of frequency, while looser rules increase activity but also noise.

Rule-based thinking is not about building static, unchangeable systems. Rules can—and should—be adapted as markets evolve, but changes must be deliberate, evidence-based, and forward-tested before full deployment. One of the most common errors in algorithmic design is retrofitting rules to past data until they "fit" perfectly, a practice known as overfitting. A rule that appears flawless on historical charts may collapse in live markets because it has been tuned to idiosyncrasies that will never repeat. This is why *if-then* thinking should be applied with a focus on robustness, not perfection. Rules must be resilient across different market regimes, not just optimised for yesterday's conditions.

The discipline of defining rules also reveals an often-overlooked advantage: transparency. An algorithm built on explicit conditions can be audited. You can trace exactly why a trade occurred, reconstruct the state of the system at that moment, and verify whether it acted within its mandate. This stands in stark contrast to discretionary trading, where post hoc rationalisations can obscure the real reasons behind a decision. Rule-based systems leave a clear trail of cause and effect, which not only aids refinement but also builds trust—both for individual operators and for stakeholders such as investors or compliance officers.

Behavioural finance provides further support for rule-based approaches. Humans are prone to a range of cognitive biases—anchoring, loss aversion, confirmation bias—that distort decision-making under uncertainty. By pre-committing to explicit rules, you shield execution from many of these biases. The algorithm cannot decide to "hold on just a little longer" because it hopes for a reversal; it cannot selectively seek information that supports an existing position. It follows the rule or it does nothing. This does not eliminate risk, but it does eliminate many unforced errors that drain returns over time.

The most effective way to approach rule creation is iterative. Begin with the simplest viable set of conditions—enough to capture the essence of your strategy without introducing unnecessary complexity. Run it on historical data to observe performance, not with the aim of fitting it to the past, but to understand its behaviour in varied conditions. From there, refine the rules incrementally, testing each change for its contribution to the system's stability and profitability. This incrementalism keeps the strategy grounded in logic rather than drifting toward elaborate constructions that look impressive in backtests but crumble in live use.

Ultimately, rule-based thinking is less about programming syntax and more about mindset. It requires you to shift from reactive, situational decision-making to proactive, premeditated design. Every "if" must have a clear rationale, every "then" a justified response. The power of the approach lies not in the sophistication of individual rules but in the consistency with which they are applied. In markets where uncertainty is the norm and emotional decision-making is costly, a well-crafted set of rules is not just a tool for automation—it is a framework for disciplined thought.

## Avoiding Overfitting

The greatest danger in algorithmic trading is not building a system that fails outright, but creating one that appears flawless—until it meets reality. Overfitting is the quiet saboteur of quantitative strategies, a trap that seduces both novices and seasoned practitioners with the illusion of perfection. It occurs when an algorithm is tuned so precisely to historical data that it captures not just the underlying patterns but also the random quirks, anomalies, and statistical noise unique to that dataset. The result is a model that excels on paper but falters the moment it encounters new conditions, because it has learned the past too well and the future not at all.

To grasp the essence of overfitting, imagine preparing for an exam by memorising every question and answer from last year's test. You might score perfectly if the same questions reappear, but your knowledge is brittle. The slightest change in wording or topic leaves you exposed. A robust study method would focus instead on the principles behind the questions, equipping you to tackle variations you've never seen. Overfitted algorithms are the memorisers of the trading world—they perform brilliantly on the specific "exam" of historical data, but are ill-prepared for the evolving and unpredictable test that is the live market.

The seduction of overfitting lies in its feedback loop. Backtesting—a critical part of any algorithm's development—can tempt designers to adjust parameters repeatedly until they produce the most impressive equity curve. Change the moving average period from 50 days to 47, adjust the stop-loss from 2.0% to 1.8%, and suddenly the system's historical performance improves dramatically. Each tweak feels rational and justified, but in aggregate they sculpt a strategy optimised for coincidences: that one unusual rally in March, that abrupt reversal in October, the specific volatility regime of a narrow historical window. These are market "accidents," not enduring truths.

Real-world cases illustrate the danger vividly. In the early 2000s, a major hedge fund deployed a high-frequency strategy that had been fine-tuned to years of back data. It produced stunning simulated returns and performed well initially in live trading. Then, within months, the strategy unravelled. Post-mortem analysis revealed that the model had been trained on a period dominated by unusually stable correlations between certain asset classes. When those correlations broke down due to macroeconomic shifts, the strategy's logic collapsed. The algorithm had mistaken a temporary historical feature for a permanent law of market behaviour.

A common misunderstanding is that overfitting can be eliminated entirely; it cannot. Any time we build a model from historical data, there is an inherent risk of embedding some noise along with the signal. The goal, therefore, is not to eradicate overfitting but to *minimise its influence* and ensure that the patterns we rely on are more likely to persist. One of the most effective tools for this is out-of-sample testing—evaluating the algorithm on data it has never "seen" during its development. If the model performs comparably well on both in-sample and out-of-sample data, it suggests that the rules capture a generalisable pattern rather than a statistical fluke.

Another safeguard is to resist the temptation of excessive complexity. It is counterintuitive, but in markets—as in many domains—simpler models often outperform more intricate ones over time. This is because every additional rule or parameter increases the model's flexibility, allowing it to fit historical data more closely but also increasing the risk that it is fitting the noise. A lean, well-justified set of rules has fewer degrees of freedom, making it harder for the model to latch onto meaningless correlations. This principle is supported not just by trading experience but by the broader scientific ethos: the more assumptions a theory requires to explain the data, the more fragile it is when conditions change.

Accessible analogies can help crystallise this. Picture a tailor crafting a suit. If the suit is cut precisely to fit the shape of one client standing perfectly still, it may look immaculate in the fitting room. But the moment the client moves, gains weight, or wears a different pair of shoes, the suit becomes uncomfortable or even unwearable. A good tailor anticipates variability—he leaves enough give in the fabric and flexibility in the design so that the garment remains functional in changing circumstances. Overfitting is the tailor who forgets that life is dynamic and designs only for a frozen moment in time.

Behavioural finance adds another layer to the discussion. The human tendency toward *outcome bias*—judging decisions by their results rather than their reasoning—drives much of the overfitting problem. When we see a backtest with high returns, we tend to overestimate its future reliability, even if those returns were the result of luck in the historical period tested. Similarly, *confirmation bias* pushes us to keep refining a model until the results match our expectations, blinding us to the fact that each adjustment may be eroding the model's real-world robustness.

In practice, the fight against overfitting requires humility. It means accepting that no algorithm will work all the time, and that the market will inevitably present scenarios your backtest never encountered. It also demands a disciplined development process: defining the strategy's rationale before running performance tests, limiting parameter adjustments, and documenting every change along with the reason for it. This documentation acts as a safeguard against the slow creep of unjustified optimisation—a subtle but pervasive threat in the iterative cycle of model building.

The irony is that the very tools that enable us to build sophisticated trading algorithms—massive datasets, high-speed computation, advanced statistical techniques—also make overfitting easier. The more granular the data and the more flexible the model, the more patterns it will find, many of which will be spurious. In this sense, restraint becomes a competitive advantage. By choosing to model only what you can reasonably explain and defend, you trade some historical performance for a much greater likelihood of surviving the future.

Ultimately, avoiding overfitting is about building algorithms that think in terms of probabilities, not certainties. Markets are adaptive systems with countless interacting variables; they cannot be reduced to a static equation without losing something essential. A strategy that survives changing volatility regimes, shifting correlations, and macroeconomic shocks will always appear less "perfect" in hindsight than one optimised for a narrow slice of history. Yet that imperfection is precisely what makes it durable. The discipline lies in resisting the siren call of the flawless backtest and embracing the messy, resilient truth of real markets.

### The Minimum Viable Algorithm

Complexity is seductive. When we first approach algorithmic trading, it is tempting to believe that a successful system must be intricate, weaving together dozens of indicators, multi-layered decision rules, and advanced statistical filters. The truth is almost always the opposite. In the early stages, complexity rarely equates to robustness; it more often reflects overconfidence, impatience, or a misunderstanding of what makes an algorithm truly effective. The most reliable way to begin is not by building the perfect system, but by developing *the simplest possible set of rules that can be tested in the real world.* This is the essence of the minimum viable algorithm.

The idea borrows from product development, where a minimum viable product is the leanest version of a concept that still delivers its core function. For trading, this means identifying the smallest number of well-defined rules that are both testable and logically grounded. A minimum viable algorithm should be so clear that you can describe its logic in one or two sentences without ambiguity. If you find yourself explaining exceptions, contingencies, and special cases before your first backtest, you have already left the minimum viable territory.

Consider a simple moving average crossover system as an example. Two moving averages—say, 50-day and 200-day—form the entire logic: buy when the shorter crosses above the longer, sell when it crosses below. Such a system is crude by modern quantitative standards, yet it contains several virtues: it is easy to explain, easy to test, and its rationale is transparent (identifying shifts in trend). More importantly, because it has so few moving parts, any performance seen in testing is less likely to be an artefact of overfitting. By contrast, a system that blends five indicators, each with multiple adjustable parameters, can generate impressive historical returns while being hopelessly fragile in the future.

The discipline of starting small forces the trader to confront the market's most essential question: does the core idea have merit? Stripping the system to its bare minimum removes the camouflage that complexity provides. If the concept fails in its simplest form, layering on refinements will only mask the weakness rather than fix it. An underpowered engine does not become high-performance simply by adding more gears.

This approach also accelerates the feedback loop between hypothesis and evidence. A minimal set of rules can be backtested, forward-tested, and evaluated quickly, enabling more cycles of iteration and learning. This is critical because markets are dynamic. Even a sound strategy will require adaptation over time, and those who reach functional prototypes faster gain a compounding advantage in refining them. In this way, the minimum viable algorithm is not just a starting point—it is a method for ongoing development.

Importantly, simplicity is not synonymous with naïveté. A well-crafted minimal algorithm should still be grounded in economic reasoning or behavioural finance principles. For example, a rule that buys after large downward price gaps in fundamentally sound stocks might be based on the documented tendency for overreactions to correct—a phenomenon supported by decades of empirical research. The key is that such logic can be tested without adding layers of conditional filters until the core premise has proven its worth.

There is also a psychological dimension. Humans are naturally inclined to add rather than subtract, especially when results are unsatisfactory. In algorithmic design, this often manifests as adding more parameters, more conditions, more data inputs in an attempt to "fix" poor performance. The minimum viable framework resists this impulse by demanding that the first iterations remain deliberately sparse. It cultivates the discipline to *remove* elements that do not contribute materially, rather than continually layering on new ones.

Real-world experience supports this philosophy. Some of the most enduring trading strategies in history—momentum, mean reversion, carry—are based on rules so straightforward they can be summarised on a single page. Their longevity comes not from hidden complexity, but from the fact that they tap into persistent drivers of market behaviour, and that they can be adapted incrementally as conditions evolve.

A further advantage of minimalism is transparency. When a strategy has only a few moving parts, it is easier to diagnose why it is working—or failing. This diagnostic clarity is essential for making informed adjustments rather than reactive ones. If your algorithm consists of three rules, and it begins underperforming, you can examine each rule in isolation and determine which is faltering. In a system with dozens of interlocking conditions, isolating the cause of underperformance becomes nearly impossible without effectively rebuilding the strategy from scratch.

Critics sometimes argue that starting with minimal rules risks underutilising the vast computational and data resources now available. But restraint is not waste; it is focus. Advanced tools should be applied to test and validate the robustness of core ideas, not to overcomplicate them before they have demonstrated resilience. The most sophisticated work in quantitative finance often happens after the initial minimal version has been proven, where refinements can be targeted and justified.

The process of moving from a minimum viable algorithm to a more mature system should be evolutionary, not revolutionary. Once the basic rules have survived initial scrutiny, improvements can be introduced gradually: refining entry and exit triggers, incorporating additional risk controls, or expanding to new asset classes. Each modification should be tested against both historical and live data to ensure that the added complexity is earning its keep. The original minimal version serves as a benchmark, a reminder of what the strategy looked like when it was at its purest and most transparent.

Ultimately, the minimum viable algorithm is a philosophy of disciplined construction. It is a safeguard against the hubris that assumes markets will reward ingenuity for its own sake. By beginning with the simplest viable expression of a trading idea, you give yourself the best chance of identifying strategies that endure beyond the backtest, survive the friction of real execution, and adapt gracefully as the market shifts. In algorithmic trading, as in architecture, the most enduring structures are those built on strong, simple foundations.

# Chapter 4
# The Human–Machine Partnership

The most effective investors of the future will not be those who can code the most complex algorithms or those who cling stubbornly to purely discretionary judgment. They will be those who master the subtle art of combining human intuition with machine precision—designing workflows where each side is deployed to do what it does best. This is not a call for compromise between competing approaches, but for an intentional architecture of decision-making in which human and machine act as complementary agents rather than as rivals. The idea is deceptively simple: algorithms should extend and enhance our capabilities, not replace them; humans should steer, not surrender. Yet in practice, achieving this balance demands intellectual discipline, self-awareness, and a clear framework for collaboration.

Part of the challenge lies in recognising the fundamental asymmetries between human and machine cognition. There remain domains where even the most sophisticated algorithms are crude approximations: weighing the moral consequences of a decision, situating events within their full cultural and historical context, or detecting when the rules themselves have shifted in ways no dataset has yet captured. Markets are not merely numerical constructs—they are social organisms. Humans retain a distinct advantage in perceiving shifts in sentiment, deciphering the subtleties of political risk, or interpreting ambiguous signals that to a machine would appear as mere noise. A trader seasoned by multiple crises often senses the early tremors of panic before they register statistically, much as a veteran sailor can feel a storm approaching long before a cloud darkens the horizon.

By contrast, there are domains where machines do not merely surpass humans—they operate in an altogether different register. The scale and velocity at which algorithms can scan, filter, and analyse market data are beyond biological comprehension. Millions of price movements, correlations, and anomalies can be evaluated in fractions of a second, without fatigue, emotional distortion, or memory bias. Machines do not forget the rules mid-trade; they do not falter in the face of sudden volatility; they do not persuade themselves to "wait a little longer" when a stop-loss ought to be executed. This unemotional consistency is as valuable as their computational power. When deployed thoughtfully, it liberates human decision-makers from the relentless cognitive burden of constant vigilance.

Friction emerges when the boundaries blur—when an algorithm's recommendation collides with human instinct. Absent a deliberate "judgment filter," decision-making becomes erratic: overrides occur either too frequently, eroding the statistical edge, or too seldom, allowing avoidable losses to accumulate. The solution is to establish, in advance, precisely defined conditions for intervention—

triggers that indicate when the machine may no longer be operating within its intended assumptions. Without such guardrails, human action risks devolving into ego-driven improvisation rather than disciplined application of expertise.

This partnership is not merely a division of labour; it is the design of an integrated workflow. In a robust routine, algorithms lead in scanning and filtering the market's noise, presenting only the most salient signals. Humans then bring context and judgment, deciding which signals warrant action and how to calibrate size and timing. This routine scales—from daily tactical choices to quarterly portfolio reviews—each component knowing its responsibilities. The benefit is more than efficiency: it reduces the likelihood of catastrophic error by ensuring that no single layer operates in isolation.

Viewed in this light, the human–machine partnership becomes a discipline of governance as much as execution. It compels the investor to articulate what they believe they understand, what they know they do not, and where they are willing to place trust in the machine's output. It demands transparency in algorithm design and humility in human oversight. The arrangement functions best when explicit, codified, and continuously refined in response to real-world feedback. The most dangerous scenario is the one that develops haphazardly—where a human believes they are "in control" but is in fact reacting impulsively to a black box whose logic they scarcely comprehend.

The enduring truth is that neither humans nor machines, in isolation, can reliably outperform in the intricate ecosystem of modern markets. Humans are imaginative yet fallible, intuitive yet inconsistent. Machines are precise yet literal, powerful yet narrow. The genuine edge arises from orchestrating their strengths into a coherent system, each compensating for the other's limitations. This chapter does not romanticise technology, nor does it overstate human judgment. Instead, it will demonstrate how to define roles, build trust, and design processes that render the partnership a true force multiplier—elevating the investor's craft beyond what either side could accomplish alone.

## What Humans Do Best

For all the computational brilliance of modern algorithms, there remain areas of decision-making where human judgment is not merely relevant but essential—domains where lived experience, ethical reasoning, and contextual understanding outperform any code. The temptation in an age of machine learning is to assume that enough data, processed at sufficient speed, will inevitably produce better answers than a human could devise. Yet markets are not closed systems governed only by mathematics; they are socio-economic ecosystems shaped by shifting narratives, unquantifiable risks, and political undercurrents. In this messy, evolving reality, humans still hold decisive advantages—advantages that are not accidental by-products of biology, but deeply embedded capabilities honed over millennia of interpreting complexity.

One of the clearest strengths lies in contextual synthesis. An algorithm can process data, but it cannot truly "understand" the broader environment in which that data sits. Consider a sudden drop in a company's share price. A machine might flag the movement, run correlations, and generate predictions based on similar historical patterns. A skilled human, however, might recall that the company's CEO has been under political scrutiny in a jurisdiction where regulatory changes are imminent, or that a recent product launch in a culturally sensitive market was met with public backlash that no numerical dataset yet captures. This capacity to integrate qualitative nuance—context not yet digitised—into the decision-making process is a human strength that remains resistant to automation. *The ability to weave disparate signals, some statistical and others experiential, into a coherent narrative is a competitive edge no server rack can replicate.*

Ethical discernment is another uniquely human domain. Financial decisions are not made in a moral vacuum; they carry consequences for employees, customers, and communities. Algorithms can be programmed to optimise for returns, risk-adjusted or otherwise, but they do not experience the ethical weight of those decisions. For instance, a model might identify a high-return opportunity in a company engaged in environmentally destructive practices. A human investor may choose to forgo the profit in favour of aligning with environmental, social, and governance (ESG) principles—not because the data says it's optimal in the short term, but because the decision aligns with long-term values and reputational considerations. This is not sentimentality; it is strategic self-awareness informed by an ethical compass. Machines can be given rules to simulate ethical behaviour, but they cannot generate the principles themselves, nor anticipate the moral backlash that might arise when a decision is technically correct but socially unacceptable.

Humans also excel in interpreting weak signals—those fragments of information too ambiguous to register as statistically significant but which, in the right hands, hint at meaningful change. In the early months of the COVID-19 outbreak, some traders noted subtle disruptions in supply chain chatter, unusual spikes in certain commodity purchases, and shifts in travel behaviour before the crisis was formally recognised by the markets. Algorithms trained on historical data had no analogue for the event and thus no predictive anchor. The humans who connected the dots did so by recognising patterns that were incomplete, unverified, and non-quantitative—precisely the type of input machines are designed to filter out as noise. This sensitivity to the not-yet-measurable is both a strength and a risk; it requires discipline to act on such insights judiciously rather than impulsively.

Another strength is adaptability under uncertainty. Algorithms are highly effective when operating within a well-defined parameter space, but when the underlying rules of the game shift abruptly—due to regime changes, technological disruption, or black swan events—humans can reframe the problem itself. A machine may continue to optimise for an obsolete metric because it cannot independently redefine its objective function. A human can stop, reassess the environment, and decide that the original goal is no longer the right one. This meta-level flexibility—the capacity not just to choose between options, but to decide which options should exist—is a profound advantage in markets that evolve faster than datasets can stabilise.

Cultural literacy and narrative interpretation further distinguish human judgement. Markets move not just on fundamentals but on the stories people tell about them. An algorithm might detect a surge in social media activity about a particular asset, but understanding whether that surge reflects genuine sentiment, orchestrated hype, or ironic detachment often requires fluency in cultural cues, language subtleties, and subtext. This is particularly true in global markets, where the same piece of news can carry radically different implications depending on local context. A human analyst with cultural expertise can interpret these differences accurately, whereas a machine might misread them entirely. *In essence, humans can read between the data points as well as between the lines.*

Finally, there is the role of trust and persuasion. Decisions in markets often involve convincing stakeholders—clients, boards, regulators—to support a course of action. This requires more than presenting data; it requires framing, empathy, and negotiation. A machine can generate a recommendation, but it cannot build the relational trust necessary to persuade others to act on it. The human ability to tailor arguments to the audience, anticipate objections, and address them in real time is not an incidental skill—it is a critical part of turning analysis into outcome.

The enduring edge, then, is not about rejecting algorithms but about recognising where human strengths are irreplaceable. *Our value lies in the intersections—where hard data meets soft judgment, where computation ends and interpretation begins, where optimisation confronts ethics.* These are the points at which human decision-makers can not only complement machines but elevate the entire decision-making process beyond the sum of its parts. In an age where machine intelligence is expanding, the future advantage will belong to those who know exactly when and why to take the wheel themselves.

## What Machines Do Best

There is a kind of intelligence that humans find difficult to sustain for long periods: relentless, high-speed, exacting in every calculation, indifferent to stress, and immune to distraction. It is here—where precision, scale, and emotionless execution matter most—that machines hold a decisive advantage. The strengths of algorithms are not merely faster versions of what humans already do; they are capabilities that operate in fundamentally different ways, often revealing patterns and efficiencies that human cognition could never uncover unaided. In finance, these strengths translate into edges that are both practical and profound, particularly in environments where the difference between success and failure can be measured in milliseconds or micro-decibels of risk.

Pattern recognition is perhaps the most celebrated of these machine capabilities. Humans are wired to notice recurring shapes, behaviours, and sequences, but our pattern recognition is bounded by cognitive bandwidth and, crucially, by bias. We tend to see patterns where none exist and overlook patterns that contradict our assumptions. Machines, on the other hand, can be trained to scan vast oceans of structured and unstructured data, identifying correlations and anomalies at a granularity impossible for human perception. A trading algorithm might detect a consistent microstructure shift in currency markets that precedes a volatility spike by a few minutes—a signal too faint for a human to notice in the noise of real-time price feeds. The sheer dimensionality of these analyses allows algorithms to operate in multi-factor spaces that no human mind could consciously navigate, considering thousands of variables simultaneously without fatigue or distraction. *In tasks where the signal is real but subtle, machines not only outperform us—they make the very act of detection possible.*

Closely tied to this is the capacity for data crunching at scale. The term is often used casually, but in finance, scale is not just about volume—it is about compression of time. A model can process decades of tick-by-tick market data in minutes, testing hypotheses across multiple asset classes and geographies, then refining them based on statistical significance. Such brute-force computation is not glamorous, but it is transformative. Without it, many of the strategies that underpin modern quantitative finance would never move beyond theory; the backtesting alone would take years of human effort. Algorithms allow for iterative experimentation at a pace that makes strategy development a living process rather than a static exercise. In markets that evolve continuously, this speed of adaptation is a strategic asset.

Another area where machines dominate is emotion-free execution. Behavioural finance has shown time and again that fear, greed, and loss aversion lead to suboptimal trading behaviour, even among seasoned professionals. The human nervous system evolved to react rapidly to threats, but the fight-or-flight mechanism is poorly suited to the probabilistic nature of markets. Algorithms, by contrast, operate without psychological baggage. They do not panic in a flash crash, nor do they become overconfident after a winning streak. They execute instructions exactly as coded, without flinching at the sight of red ink or becoming seduced by the prospect of outsized gains. This discipline is not merely about avoiding mistakes; it enables strategies that rely on consistent, unemotional application over long timeframes—strategies that would be nearly impossible for a human to follow faithfully in the face of real-world volatility.

Machines also excel at operational consistency. Markets are increasingly global, running on overlapping time zones with minimal downtime. For a human trader, maintaining constant vigilance across sessions is physically and mentally exhausting. An algorithm can operate continuously, scanning for opportunities, monitoring risk parameters, and executing trades without pause. The ability to maintain perfect attention for as long as required is not just efficient—it's defensive. Many market losses occur not because the analysis was wrong, but because the window for action was missed. Algorithms close that window almost entirely.

Furthermore, machines can integrate data sources that are too disparate or complex for manual analysis. Satellite imagery of retail car parks, shipping traffic data, corporate filings, social sentiment, weather forecasts—all of these can be ingested, cleaned, and analysed by algorithms to produce actionable insights. While humans can conceive of using such data, the actual integration and weighting of these heterogeneous streams require computational methods far beyond our manual capacity. The competitive edge here is not only in the speed of analysis but in the ability to meaningfully combine data types that appear unrelated on the surface yet reveal predictive relationships when processed together.

Importantly, machines can also operate effectively in environments where reaction time itself is the edge. High-frequency trading is the most obvious example, where profits may depend on executing an order a few microseconds ahead of competitors. This is a domain where human involvement in the execution loop is not simply suboptimal—it is impossible. Algorithms here function not as tools but as autonomous actors, engaging in competitive interactions with other machines in a realm where latency, co-location, and hardware optimisation define the battlefield.

However, the power of these capabilities is not absolute; it is contingent on the quality of the data, the soundness of the model, and the appropriateness of the task. Machines excel when the rules of engagement are relatively stable, the objective is well-defined, and the environment can be sufficiently described by measurable inputs. They are unmatched at finding patterns in structured environments and executing decisions derived from them without hesitation. But their very strengths—relentless consistency, unblinking adherence to rules, inability to reinterpret objectives—can become limitations when the environment shifts in ways the system was not designed to accommodate. This is why the most effective use of machines in markets does not seek to replace human judgment, but to anchor it in a foundation of precise, scalable, and unbiased computational power.

*When tasks demand processing complexity at a scale that human minds cannot sustain, or require execution at speeds humans cannot approach, the machine's superiority is not up for debate—it is structural.* The art lies in knowing which parts of the process belong in silicon and which must remain in flesh and blood. Those who master this division of labour gain not only the efficiencies of automation but also the resilience of hybrid decision-making—one where each component plays to its unique strengths, and the whole is far greater than either could achieve alone.

### The Judgment Filter

The paradox of algorithmic investing is that its greatest strength—relentless adherence to predefined rules—can also be its most dangerous weakness. Markets are living systems, not mechanical puzzles. They change regime, produce events that no backtest anticipated, and are occasionally gripped by forces that break statistical relationships that once seemed immutable. In such moments, the human role is not to second-guess every line of code, but to know precisely *when* the code must be overruled. This is the essence of the judgment filter: a disciplined, clearly defined process for deciding when to step outside the algorithm's recommendation and take responsibility for a different course of action. Without it, human intervention tends to devolve into reactive meddling; with it, intervention becomes an informed, high-conviction act.

The need for a judgment filter becomes evident when we recognise that all models are simplifications. By design, an algorithm strips away what it cannot quantify, reducing reality to variables it can measure, process, and act upon. That reduction is both its strength and its Achilles' heel. A macroeconomic shock, a sudden regulatory change, or a geopolitical flashpoint may fall entirely outside its informational horizon, not because the event is unknowable, but because it was never parameterised into the system. A human can see the broader context—the lived reality of the moment—and appreciate the relevance of factors that have yet to register in the model. *The filter exists to catch those out-of-sample moments before they inflict unnecessary damage.*

A robust judgment filter starts with an acknowledgement of the scenarios in which human intuition, context, and ethical reasoning are structurally superior to computational output. For instance, a sudden suspension of trading in a major security due to regulatory investigation will not initially appear in the algorithm's historical price-based logic. Left unchecked, the system may continue to recommend positions that are, in practical terms, unexecutable or catastrophically risky. Likewise, an algorithm that trades agricultural commodities based on seasonal patterns may continue buying contracts in the midst of a rare but catastrophic crop disease outbreak—an event whose implications a human could infer instantly from news headlines. These are situations where the "if-then" rules that govern the machine's decision-making have not yet been updated to reflect new conditions, and where human override is not only justified but essential.

However, the most effective judgment filters are not built on a vague sense of "I'll know it when I see it." They require explicit criteria for intervention—thresholds that, once crossed, trigger a review. These criteria might be quantitative, such as a volatility spike exceeding a defined multiple of the strategy's backtested range, or qualitative, such as an unprecedented policy announcement from a central bank. The purpose of codifying them is not to eliminate human discretion, but to channel it. *Without predefined triggers, human override risks becoming a steady drip of bias into the system, degrading the very discipline the algorithm was designed to enforce.*

This brings us to one of the central tensions in applying the judgment filter: the trade-off between agility and consistency. Intervene too rarely, and you risk letting the model sail straight into an iceberg it cannot see. Intervene too often, and you undermine the statistical edge of the system, replacing it with the well-documented pitfalls of discretionary trading—overreaction, recency bias, and loss aversion. This is why the filter is not a licence for improvisation; it is a structured checkpoint that operates on clearly defined triggers, ideally agreed upon in advance during the strategy design phase.

Case studies from professional trading desks illustrate both the power and the pitfalls of judgment filtering. In 2015, during the Swiss National Bank's sudden removal of its franc-to-euro cap, algorithms tied to currency pairs suffered devastating losses if left unchecked. The most resilient firms were those whose traders had authority to immediately suspend automated execution upon the announcement, recognising the magnitude of the policy shift before the market fully absorbed it. Conversely, in more benign cases—such as temporary volatility surges following minor political events—overrides have been shown to erode returns, as traders aborted positions that would have recovered within hours had the system been left alone. The lesson is that judgment must be rare enough to preserve the algorithm's statistical reliability, but swift and decisive when the world delivers a shock the model was never designed to process.

Another dimension of the judgment filter is ethics. Algorithms are indifferent to the moral or reputational implications of their trades; they optimise for the objective encoded in them. Yet investors operate in a world where optics, stakeholder relations, and long-term trust matter. An algorithm may identify profitable short positions in the shares of a company at the centre of a humanitarian crisis—but executing those trades may be reputationally corrosive or ethically unacceptable for the investor. Here, the judgment filter serves not only as a guard against financial harm, but as a safeguard for institutional values. Ethical overrides should be as deliberate and codified as risk-based ones, ensuring that they are applied consistently rather than on impulse.

Designing a judgment filter also demands clarity about roles and responsibilities. Who has the authority to intervene, and under what conditions? How is that decision documented? In institutional settings, this may involve a formal escalation path, where an intervention is logged, justified, and reviewed post hoc. In individual trading, it may mean keeping a written decision journal that forces the trader to articulate the rationale for overriding the model in real time. These records serve two purposes: they create accountability, and they provide valuable data for refining both the algorithm and the judgment filter itself. Patterns in override decisions may reveal blind spots in the model or biases in the human operator that need addressing.

Ultimately, the judgment filter is about balance. The machine brings consistency, precision, and scalability; the human brings context, adaptability, and values. The filter is the mechanism that decides when the latter must take precedence over the former, without allowing either to dominate to the point of dysfunction. Its existence acknowledges a simple truth: the market is too complex for either human or machine to master alone. The investor who can define, trust, and execute their judgment filter will not only avoid catastrophic missteps—they will build a partnership between human and algorithm that is resilient, principled, and capable of thriving in conditions that defeat purely automated or purely discretionary approaches.

## Designing Your Workflow

The most successful investors who blend human judgment with algorithmic power do not treat the machine as a novelty or an occasional advisor. They weave it into a deliberate, repeatable routine that defines when and how decisions are made. Without structure, algorithms risk being either overused—blindly followed without oversight—or underused, sidelined in favour of impulsive human judgement. The aim is neither automation for its own sake nor a return to gut-led trading, but a *workflow that allocates cognitive and mechanical labour to the domain where each is strongest*. This requires both architectural thinking and operational discipline.

The first principle in designing such a workflow is temporal clarity: knowing which decisions should be made daily, which weekly, and which only in response to specific triggers. Algorithms excel in *continuous vigilance*—they can process tick-by-tick market data, scanning for patterns or anomalies without fatigue. Humans, by contrast, cannot and should not attempt to replicate that pace. Instead, human involvement is best scheduled for moments that require contextual interpretation or discretionary calls that affect the strategic trajectory of the portfolio. A disciplined investor might, for example, review algorithmic signals once per day at a set hour, ensuring decisions are made in a controlled state of mind, rather than in the heat of market noise. Weekly reviews might then focus on performance drift, risk exposures, and any structural changes in the market environment that the model is not designed to detect.

A coherent workflow also addresses *decision hierarchy*. Not all outputs from an algorithm deserve equal attention or action. Some signals are designed for automatic execution, with minimal human involvement unless they breach a predefined risk threshold. Others are advisory—flagging conditions that may warrant human discretion but do not mandate it. The key is to pre-classify which categories fall under which rule set, so that human oversight is not arbitrary but applied where it adds genuine value. Without this premeditation, investors often fall into the trap of "selective listening," acting on the algorithm's advice only when it happens to agree with their pre-existing bias, thereby corrupting both the system and the process.

One of the most overlooked elements of workflow design is *information sequencing*. The order in which an investor is exposed to data and recommendations shapes their interpretation. If you begin the day by looking at the algorithm's suggested trades before reviewing macroeconomic developments, you risk interpreting the news through the lens of the model's positioning rather than evaluating the model's positioning in light of the news. Inverting this sequence can fundamentally alter the quality of judgment. The most effective workflows choreograph information exposure to avoid anchoring bias, ensuring that human insight is formed independently before being compared with algorithmic outputs.

Consider the example of a professional commodities trader who uses an algorithm to track global shipping data, weather forecasts, and supply-demand imbalances. The algorithm runs constantly, but its output is not streamed to the trader in real time. Instead, the trader receives a curated daily digest at a fixed hour, showing only actionable signals that meet predefined thresholds. This is followed by a brief period of discretionary analysis where the trader integrates qualitative intelligence—conversations with suppliers, regional news reports, political developments—before making a final decision. By structuring the process in this way, the trader avoids the constant drip of noise while still harnessing the algorithm's real-time scanning power.

To sustain such a workflow over the long term, *feedback loops* are essential. Every human override, delayed execution, or adjustment to algorithmic output should be documented, along with the rationale. Over time, these records form a goldmine for refining both the model and the workflow itself. Patterns may emerge: perhaps overrides during periods of high volatility add value, while overrides during quiet markets consistently reduce performance. These insights allow the workflow to evolve in an evidence-based manner, gradually shifting the human–machine balance toward its most productive state.

An effective workflow also respects *cognitive ergonomics*. Just as a physical workspace can be optimised for comfort and efficiency, so too can the decision environment. If reviewing algorithmic outputs is consistently the last task of a mentally draining day, the likelihood of errors or impulsive overrides rises sharply. Structuring reviews for times when focus and energy are highest can significantly improve the quality of interaction with the machine. Similarly, separating the physical or digital spaces where analysis and execution occur can reduce the temptation to act on unvalidated hunches.

The allocation of algorithmic and human tasks within a workflow must also acknowledge the *limits of each domain*. Algorithms can monitor hundreds of securities simultaneously, detect micro-patterns invisible to the naked eye, and execute trades with precision in milliseconds. They are invaluable in environments where speed and consistency are paramount. Humans, however, are better at integrating unstructured information, interpreting ambiguous developments, and making value-based decisions. A resilient workflow ensures that neither is forced into a role for which it is ill-suited. This is why some of the most effective investment operations resemble a relay race: the algorithm handles the opening leg—scanning, filtering, and ranking opportunities—before handing off to the human for contextual judgment and final execution.

A final but crucial consideration in workflow design is *resilience under stress*. Market crises are precisely when workflows are most likely to break down, as emotions surge and pressure to act becomes acute. Yet these are also the moments when a well-structured workflow delivers its greatest value, providing a stabilising routine in chaotic conditions. Building in predefined crisis protocols—such as halting certain automated trades when liquidity evaporates, or shifting to manual review during news-driven volatility—ensures that the partnership between human and machine does not disintegrate under strain.

In essence, designing your workflow is about creating a repeatable architecture for decision-making that respects the comparative advantages of both human and machine. It is about deciding *in advance* how information flows, when human judgment intervenes, and how actions are documented and reviewed. The best workflows are not rigid bureaucracies; they are living systems that adapt as both the market and the investor's tools evolve. They allow the machine to shoulder the burden of relentless monitoring, rapid computation, and bias-free execution, while preserving the human's role as strategist, contextual interpreter, and ethical compass. In doing so, they transform the human–machine relationship from a loose collaboration into a disciplined, high-performance partnership—one that is not only more efficient, but more resilient, than either party could achieve alone.

# Chapter 5
# Choosing the Right Tools Without Getting Scammed

If the past twenty years of financial technology have demonstrated anything, it is that innovation seldom arrives neatly packaged or pre-validated. It tends to appear in a jumble of promise, hype, opportunism, and, occasionally, outright deception. The surge of retail-accessible AI trading platforms is a striking example of this chaotic pattern. Once the exclusive domain of hedge funds and proprietary trading desks—where algorithmic analytics, machine learning pattern recognition, and real-time risk modelling were the norm—these capabilities now glitter across glossy dashboards, subscription offers, and browser-based tools pitched to everyday investors. Yet accessibility has not translated into discernment. The retail marketplace often resembles a frontier economy, where genuine innovation vies for attention against hastily assembled imitations, white-labelled software sold under inflated branding, and, at the extreme, tools designed more to extract value from users than to provide it. Navigating this terrain demands more than technical literacy; it requires the scepticism of a seasoned investor, the instinct for verification of a journalist, and the strategic clarity to distinguish needs from wants.

The diversity of available tools only complicates matters. For every platform with a transparent methodology, well-documented performance data, and robust user support, there are several more that lean heavily on marketing polish while revealing little about actual functionality. It is not uncommon to encounter services promising AI-driven "certainty" in markets—a phrase that should instantly trigger caution for anyone acquainted with market realities. Others offer real-time insights yet rely on outdated or incomplete data feeds, undermining their very premise. The gap between marketing narrative and practical utility can be wide enough to render a tool ineffective—or, worse, dangerously misleading. In such a crowded landscape, it is easy for investors, particularly those without technical backgrounds, to mistake polish for competence or popularity for reliability.

The challenge is compounded by the psychological pressures intrinsic to trading. A platform claiming to neutralise uncertainty is appealing not only intellectually, but emotionally. During periods of volatility, retail investors may be drawn to tools that promise predictive precision, especially when presented with slick interfaces and seemingly credible endorsements. The risk is not only financial loss but the erosion of critical judgement, as decisions shift from careful analysis to fear-driven impulse. This is precisely how predatory actors gain traction: offering solutions that appear to simplify markets, framing them as solvable puzzles accessible via the right subscription.

Selecting the right tool, therefore, is about far more than comparing features. It is about establishing a set of core criteria—non-negotiable filters through which any candidate must pass. Transparency comes first: if a platform cannot explain, even at a high level, how it generates insights, the user is effectively buying into a black box. Usability is not a matter of aesthetic minimalism, but whether the interface supports informed decision-making without obscuring critical data. Support is likewise more than a responsive help desk; it encompasses comprehensive documentation, educational resources, and an active community where substantive answers are provided rather than platitudes. A platform meeting these criteria is no guarantee of market-beating returns, but it clears the baseline threshold of legitimacy and functionality.

Whether to pay for such tools or rely on free alternatives is a matter of trade-offs rather than ideology. Paid platforms often promise richer datasets, advanced analytics, and proprietary models. Some deliver, others simply place a paywall before features available elsewhere at no cost. Conversely, many robust tools—particularly in data visualisation and backtesting—are open-source or supported by academic and non-profit initiatives. Their sophistication can rival, and occasionally exceed, commercial counterparts. The distinction lies not in the price tag but in alignment with the investor's objectives. A professional managing a large portfolio may gain from premium data feeds offering millisecond latency advantages; a part-time retail investor is unlikely to benefit meaningfully from the same feature.

Identifying red flags extends beyond obvious scams. The latter—unsolicited emails, unrealistic return claims, poorly written websites—are usually straightforward to detect. The more insidious threats arise from platforms that maintain an appearance of professionalism while embedding practices that disadvantage users: vague terms of service, fee structures incentivising excessive trading, cherry-picked backtest metrics, or improperly sourced data. Such sophistication can catch even experienced investors off guard if approached without a disciplined evaluation framework.

Ultimately, choosing the right tools is as much about process as product. In a landscape where the lines between cutting-edge and counterfeit blur, the ability to separate substance from surface constitutes the investor's real edge. It is the difference between constructing a technology stack that genuinely amplifies decision quality and becoming another cautionary tale of how marketing exploits naivety. This chapter aims to cultivate that edge—not through exhaustive catalogues of tools, which are obsolete almost immediately, but via enduring principles and evaluative habits that remain valid regardless of how the marketplace evolves. By its conclusion, the reader should be equipped not merely to choose wisely today, but to maintain discernment as tools—and the tactics used to sell them—inevitably change.

## The Wild West of Retail AI Tools

The retail AI trading space has expanded so quickly that its boundaries are still ill-defined, a territory marked more by speed than by regulation, more by marketing intensity than by proven capability. In the past, algorithmic trading was the domain of highly specialised financial institutions with access to expensive infrastructure, proprietary datasets, and teams of quantitative analysts. Now, a retail investor with nothing more than a laptop and an internet connection can subscribe to an algorithmic platform that promises to deliver "hedge fund–level intelligence" for a modest monthly fee. This democratisation of access is often presented as an unambiguous positive, but the reality is that it has created an ecosystem where genuine breakthroughs and empty promises sit side by side, indistinguishable to the untrained eye. The rapid commercialisation of AI in retail investing has given rise to a market that, for all its sophistication in presentation, is structurally similar to speculative frontiers in history—lucrative for those selling the tools, hazardous for those rushing in without a map.

The hype is not accidental. Companies in this space compete not only on technical merit but on narrative—how effectively they can frame their product as the key to unlocking a competitive edge in unpredictable markets. This has produced a flood of platforms with glossy branding, impressive-sounding claims, and backtest results that suggest uncanny accuracy. The problem is that much of this precision exists only in the past tense. Backtests are easily optimised to perform spectacularly on historical data, yet crumble under the pressure of live markets. And because most retail users lack the means to independently verify these claims, they are left to rely on trust—or more often, on the persuasive power of well-crafted marketing copy. *The result is a marketplace where the most visible platforms are not necessarily the most capable, and where sophistication in design often masks simplicity in function.*

If the early internet had its dot-com bubble, the retail AI space is experiencing a similar dynamic—though without the same level of institutional oversight or investor due diligence. Start-ups and established players alike are racing to capture market share, sometimes prioritising speed of launch over rigorous product validation. Features are rolled out in beta states, with paying users acting as the de facto quality assurance team. This creates a paradox: the very audience that these tools are supposed to empower ends up bearing the cost—both financial and strategic—of their imperfections. Yet the scarcity mindset induced by marketing ("limited slots available," "join the elite early adopters") often pushes users into commitments before they have had time to evaluate whether the tool offers genuine utility.

Some of the most aggressive entrants in this field position their platforms as all-in-one solutions, capable of data gathering, analysis, trade execution, and portfolio management. While such integration can be beneficial, it also increases user dependence on a single provider, amplifying the risk if the platform's algorithms underperform or if the company itself lacks financial stability. Others opt for a narrower value proposition—focusing on signal generation, for example—but rely on datasets of unknown quality, sometimes repackaging freely available public data while charging premium subscription rates. The opacity surrounding data sources, model architecture, and testing methodology is one of the most consistent patterns in the space, and one that leaves users unable to distinguish between tools built on robust foundations and those assembled from off-the-shelf components.

There is also a growing tension between usability and transparency. Platforms aimed at beginners often prioritise visual simplicity—colour-coded trade signals, clean dashboards, and minimal technical jargon. While this lowers the barrier to entry, it can come at the expense of user understanding. The risk is that the investor becomes a passive executor of algorithmic instructions without grasping the assumptions or limitations embedded in those recommendations. At the other end of the spectrum, highly technical platforms provide transparency through complexity—offering detailed logs, model parameters, and statistical outputs that overwhelm all but the most experienced quants. In both cases, the gap between presentation and comprehension remains, and without deliberate effort from the user to bridge it, the advantage of the technology is only partially realised.

An additional complication is the speed with which trends ripple through the marketplace. A particular modelling approach—say, sentiment analysis on financial news—can become the dominant selling point across dozens of platforms within months. The replication is often superficial: the underlying algorithms may differ little from basic natural language processing scripts available in open-source libraries, yet are marketed as proprietary breakthroughs. This imitation cycle creates a feedback loop where competitive differentiation narrows, and the battle shifts from engineering performance to marketing persuasion. The consequence is a market where *perceived novelty often outpaces actual innovation*.

Regulation, at present, offers little protection to retail users. While financial authorities in major markets have begun scrutinising AI-assisted trading products, most oversight focuses on institutional-grade systems or explicitly fraudulent schemes. The grey zone occupied by retail platforms—where exaggeration is artfully kept just short of outright deception—remains largely untouched. This lack of formal guardrails places the burden of due diligence squarely on the user, who must learn to evaluate technical claims, understand the limitations of machine learning in trading, and interpret the difference between genuine performance data and marketing artefacts.

Yet it would be a mistake to dismiss the entire sector as smoke and mirrors. Embedded within this crowded, hype-saturated space are platforms of genuine capability, often developed by small, technically rigorous teams who prioritise accuracy over reach. These tools may not have the marketing budgets of their flashier competitors, but they tend to demonstrate more modest, evidence-based claims and often encourage users to experiment with and validate their strategies. The challenge for the investor is that these high-quality offerings can be hard to identify, particularly when they are outshouted by the noise of aggressive advertising.

In this environment, discernment becomes the critical skill. The investor must learn to look past the surface appeal of promotional material and to ask questions that probe the architecture, data integrity, and testing methodology of the tool. They must resist the psychological pull of exclusivity and urgency, recognising these as sales tactics rather than indicators of capability. And they must acknowledge that in a space as dynamic and unregulated as this one, no tool—regardless of its sophistication—removes the need for human oversight and judgement. The true hazard of the Wild West is not the existence of bad actors, but the willingness of good actors to rely on the same persuasive mechanisms, making it harder for even the careful observer to tell the difference.

The retail AI tool market will mature. History suggests that consolidation, increased regulation, and user sophistication will eventually separate sustainable innovations from opportunistic ventures. But until that point, investors navigating this terrain are best served by approaching it with a dual mindset: open to the genuine advances that can improve decision-making, yet sceptical enough to challenge every claim before it shapes their capital allocation. In a marketplace where speed and spectacle often outpace rigour, the ability to discern substance from showmanship is the most valuable algorithm you can develop for yourself.

## Core Criteria for Selection

The most sophisticated algorithm is of little value if it is deployed through a platform that is opaque, poorly supported, or fundamentally misaligned with the user's needs. In the crowded and often noisy marketplace of retail AI tools, evaluating platforms is not merely a matter of comparing advertised features; it is an exercise in assessing integrity, usability, and resilience. The difference between a tool that becomes an enduring asset and one that drains both capital and confidence lies less in technical specifications alone and more in how those specifications are delivered, supported, and made accountable. This is why *transparency, usability, and support* form the non-negotiable triad for any serious evaluation.

Transparency is the first filter, and perhaps the most easily compromised in the race for commercial advantage. In practice, it means more than an abstract commitment to openness; it is evidenced by clear documentation, verifiable performance records, and an honest account of the tool's limitations. A credible platform should be willing to detail the scope of its data sources—whether proprietary, purchased, or public—and explain the processes through which data is cleaned, validated, and integrated into the algorithmic models. Equally, it should provide insight into the architecture of those models, not necessarily revealing every line of proprietary code but at least describing the methodology, assumptions, and statistical frameworks that underpin their operation. The absence of such information is a warning sign, and one that should carry more weight in decision-making than even the most persuasive marketing language. *A user who cannot understand the logic of their tools is trading blindfolded, regardless of how advanced the underlying technology may be.*

Transparency also extends to performance reporting. It is not enough for a platform to showcase selected historical trades with impressive returns; credible evaluation requires full backtest data, forward performance reports, and clarity on whether these results include transaction costs, slippage, and market impact. The most reliable platforms often display results that look unremarkable at first glance—steady, moderate gains without the sharp spikes of extraordinary wins—because they reflect the realities of live trading rather than the optimised artefacts of curve-fitted models. In this respect, scepticism becomes a protective skill: if the performance curve is unnaturally smooth or disproportionately steep, the prudent assumption is that the system has been over-engineered to past data.

If transparency safeguards against misplaced trust, usability ensures that a platform's potential can be realised in practice. A system can be mathematically elegant and statistically robust, yet rendered ineffective if its interface is cluttered, unintuitive, or forces the user through complex operational steps under time-sensitive conditions. Usability is not synonymous with simplicity—serious tools will inevitably involve complexity—but the best platforms channel that complexity into layers, allowing new users to operate effectively at a basic level while enabling advanced users to dig deeper without obstruction. This layering is often visible in thoughtful interface design, logical workflows, and the presence of customisation options that accommodate different trading styles without forcing a rigid operational model.

Usability also involves reliability under real market conditions. Live execution environments are dynamic, with price data updating by the second, liquidity fluctuating, and market sentiment shifting rapidly. A platform that lags during high volatility, freezes under heavy data loads, or fails to execute trades at specified trigger points is not merely inconvenient—it actively erodes the strategic edge the algorithm is meant to provide. Testing a tool under simulated stress conditions, or even during periods of market turbulence in a demo account, can reveal far more about its usability than any set of screenshots or promotional videos.

Support is the third pillar, and in many ways the one that determines whether transparency and usability can be maintained over time. Algorithmic trading platforms are not static products; they require continual updates to maintain compatibility with data feeds, exchanges, and evolving market structures. Strong support means responsive customer service, accessible technical assistance, and a development team that is actively engaged in refining and improving the tool rather than merely keeping it functional. The best providers treat their user base not as a passive revenue stream but as a source of feedback, integrating constructive suggestions into product iterations and providing clear communication about updates, fixes, and known issues.

Support is also a measure of accountability. In an industry where failed trades can be blamed on market conditions, user error, or "unexpected" events, a credible platform does not hide behind these explanations but works to investigate, explain, and resolve technical failures with documented transparency. The responsiveness and competence of support staff during the onboarding process is often a preview of how the company will behave when the stakes are higher. A user who struggles to get a prompt, informed response before subscribing is unlikely to receive better treatment once their payment is processed.

While transparency, usability, and support can be assessed individually, their real power emerges when they are considered together. A platform with excellent usability but poor transparency risks fostering dependency without understanding. One that is transparent but hard to use may be theoretically valuable yet practically inaccessible to the average investor. A tool that is both transparent and usable but unsupported will inevitably degrade over time as market conditions evolve. The investor's task is to identify the rare combination where all three criteria reinforce one another, producing a tool that is not only technically sound but operationally and strategically sustainable.

Applying these criteria requires patience and deliberate testing. Rather than committing fully to a platform based on initial impressions or promotional offers, it is often more effective to run a small-scale trial—evaluating not only the algorithm's performance but the ease of interaction, the clarity of information provided, and the responsiveness of the support team when small, non-critical issues are raised. In this way, weaknesses are exposed in a controlled context rather than during a high-stakes trading decision. The point is not to eliminate risk—no tool can do that—but to ensure that the risk you take is informed and proportional.

In a marketplace where novelty and speed are often mistaken for innovation, *discipline in platform selection becomes a strategic edge in itself*. Transparency ensures you understand the tool, usability ensures you can wield it effectively, and support ensures it evolves with you. Without all three, even the most promising algorithms risk becoming liabilities, consuming attention and capital while delivering less than they promised. With them, you acquire not just a piece of technology but a sustainable partner in the pursuit of market advantage.

## Paid vs. Free Solutions

The assumption that financial sophistication necessarily demands expensive tools is one of the most persistent misconceptions in modern investing. While it is true that certain high-performance platforms justify their price through capabilities unavailable elsewhere, it is equally true that some free solutions rival—occasionally even exceed—the functional depth and reliability of their paid counterparts. The decision to invest in a platform is therefore not a simple binary of "you get what you pay for" versus "why pay when you can get it free," but rather a matter of aligning cost with actual, measurable value in your trading process. *The most expensive mistake a retail investor can make is not overpaying—it is paying for something they neither use fully nor truly need.*

Paid platforms often differentiate themselves through access to proprietary data sources, advanced execution algorithms, and integration with professional-grade analytics. A well-constructed paid service may aggregate real-time order book depth from multiple exchanges, offer millisecond-level backtesting, or provide execution algorithms designed to minimise market impact for large trades—features that, in certain strategies, can directly translate to improved performance. There is also the less tangible but nonetheless critical value of professional support. Many reputable paid services include direct access to technical teams, priority issue resolution, and dedicated onboarding to ensure that users are not merely buying a licence but acquiring the ability to deploy the tool effectively. In environments where time is a decisive factor, this access can be worth as much as, or more than, the technology itself.

However, the presence of a price tag is not an assurance of superiority. In the retail AI marketplace, many paid platforms rely heavily on marketing sheen, bundling together freely available datasets and open-source code under a proprietary interface, then charging a premium for convenience. This can be worthwhile for traders who prioritise ease of use over technical control, but it is essential to recognise that *paying for something that exists elsewhere at no cost should be a deliberate choice, not an unwitting one.* A disciplined evaluation requires comparing not only the features offered but the provenance of those features—

whether they originate from unique intellectual property or simply a rebranded version of public-domain resources.

Free solutions, when chosen wisely, can serve as formidable trading tools. Open-source charting software such as TradingView's basic tier, coupled with freely available economic calendars, sentiment trackers, and API access to market data from certain exchanges, allows for sophisticated analysis at zero cost. Platforms like QuantConnect and Backtrader provide powerful algorithmic backtesting environments without licensing fees, drawing on a global community of contributors who continuously refine and expand their functionality. In some cases, these free ecosystems evolve faster than their paid competitors precisely because they are unconstrained by the commercial incentives that can cause vendors to lock features behind subscription tiers.

The real strength of free tools lies in their transparency. Open-source code can be examined, modified, and audited, reducing the risk of hidden processes or unexplained model behaviours. This can be particularly important for traders who value full control over their strategy logic and want to avoid the "black box" problem common in commercial products. Furthermore, free tools often foster collaborative learning: active user communities exchange scripts, strategies, and troubleshooting advice in public forums, creating a body of shared knowledge that is difficult for paid services to replicate without charging for access.

Yet the free model comes with its own costs—measured not in currency but in time and skill. Without paid support teams, users must be prepared to troubleshoot independently, interpret sometimes sparse documentation, and stay abreast of software updates that may not be communicated in a centralised manner. For those with limited technical experience, the learning curve can be steep enough to negate the theoretical savings. Additionally, free tools may lack the legal and operational infrastructure—such as service-level agreements—that guarantee uptime, security patches, and compliance with evolving financial regulations.

The most sophisticated retail investors often adopt a hybrid approach, leveraging free tools where they are genuinely competitive and supplementing them with paid services where they confer an unambiguous advantage. A trader might, for instance, use an open-source backtesting framework for model development while subscribing to a paid data feed that ensures access to clean, high-frequency tick data unavailable in the public domain. Similarly, they might rely on free charting for exploratory analysis but pay for a platform with integrated execution algorithms that can route orders optimally across fragmented markets. This hybridisation reduces dependency on any single vendor and forces a conscious evaluation of what each expense is delivering in tangible terms.

The decision between paid and free solutions should be driven by *marginal utility*—the incremental benefit derived from each additional unit of cost. For example, if a free tool enables you to implement 80% of your trading strategy effectively, the question is not whether a paid tool could take you to 100%, but whether the extra 20% justifies the financial outlay when weighed against potential returns. This requires honest assessment not just of the platform's capabilities but of your own trading style, capital base, and tolerance for operational complexity.

In certain cases, paying more can paradoxically reduce performance if it encourages over-reliance on complex features that distract from the core discipline of executing a well-tested strategy. Conversely, clinging to free tools for ideological reasons can impose opportunity costs if they lack functions that would materially improve results. The point is not to moralise about the virtues of "free" or the prestige of "paid," but to recognise that *cost efficiency in trading tools is not about minimising expenditure—it is about optimising it.*

The modern trading environment offers an unprecedented spectrum of choice, from entirely free, community-driven platforms to premium services priced at thousands of pounds per month. Navigating this spectrum demands not only technical evaluation but also strategic self-awareness. The best tool for you is not the one with the most features, the highest price, or the most vocal user base—it is the one that delivers the most consistent, measurable improvement to your trading process relative to its cost, in money, time, and cognitive load. Those who approach the paid-versus-free question with this clarity find that the market's apparent complexity reduces to a simple guiding principle: pay for what you cannot efficiently replicate yourself, and master for free what others pay to have done for them.

## Spotting Red Flags

The uncomfortable truth is that the algorithmic trading tools industry is not just populated by visionary engineers and credible fintech innovators—it is also fertile ground for opportunists, hype merchants, and outright fraudsters. The same technological revolution that has democratised access to sophisticated market analytics has also lowered the barriers for bad actors to design convincing interfaces, package recycled datasets, and market them to retail investors with the seductive promise of certainty in a world where none exists. *Recognising these red flags is not simply a matter of avoiding embarrassment; it is a fundamental skill for safeguarding capital, time, and trust.*

One of the clearest signals of a problematic platform is the use of guarantees in a domain that, by its nature, offers none. The language may be explicit—"guaranteed returns" or "risk-free profits"—or it may be cloaked in softer marketing phrases such as "consistently outperforming the market" or "proven to double your capital." In regulated jurisdictions, such claims would breach compliance guidelines outright, but the global, digital nature of the marketplace allows many operators to base themselves in permissive or loosely policed territories. A sophisticated retail investor learns to recognise not only the illegal absolutes but also the carefully worded insinuations that suggest inevitability where only probability exists.

Another hallmark of predatory marketing is the deliberate use of opacity. While not every algorithmic platform can or should disclose its full source code—proprietary intellectual property does have legitimate commercial value—there is a difference between protecting IP and hiding basic operational logic. A legitimate provider can clearly explain what inputs its models consume, the general type of algorithms it employs (for instance, statistical arbitrage, momentum analysis, or sentiment modelling), and how those algorithms are tested before deployment. By contrast, fraudulent operators often rely on vague buzzwords—"next-generation AI," "quantum analysis," "neural optimisation"—without offering any concrete description of process, validation, or risk parameters. *If you cannot discern, in plain language, what the tool is doing, it is not because it is too complex—it is because the provider has no interest in telling you.*

Equally dangerous are platforms that lean heavily on personality cults. The use of a charismatic founder or "star trader" figure is a powerful marketing lever, particularly in an industry where most retail investors feel underconfident in their technical skills. Such figures often appear in polished videos demonstrating supposed live trades, discussing their proprietary techniques, and framing the platform as an extension of their personal genius. The danger lies in the asymmetry of information: the public cannot verify whether these individuals have real track records, whether the trades shown are cherry-picked, or whether the person in the videos has any genuine connection to the underlying platform. History offers no shortage of examples—from boiler-room operations to social media "gurus"—where the cult of personality was used to mask structural deceit.

Time pressure is another favourite tactic of the dubious operator. Scarcity and urgency are potent psychological triggers, and fraudulent platforms frequently deploy them in their sales funnels: "Only 100 licences available at this price," "Sign up before midnight to secure your access," or "The next bull cycle starts in days—don't miss it." A credible provider does not need to strong-arm prospects into quick commitments; they recognise that due diligence is part of any responsible investment process and allow prospective clients the time to compare alternatives, review documentation, and test their offering under trial conditions. *The more urgently you are told to decide, the more certain you can be that the urgency serves them, not you.*

A subtler but equally revealing red flag is the over-reliance on backtested results without corresponding live performance data. Backtesting is an essential component of any algorithmic strategy's development, but it is also highly malleable: results can be selectively optimised, parameters tuned to fit past data perfectly (a practice known as overfitting), and unprofitable timeframes quietly omitted. A trustworthy platform will present backtesting alongside forward-testing or live results and will be explicit about the limitations of historical simulation. By contrast, operators engaged in deception will often present flawless equity curves, dramatic compounded returns, and smooth, drawdown-free growth without acknowledging that such perfection is virtually impossible in actual trading conditions.

Customer reviews and testimonials, while seemingly a form of social proof, can be among the most manipulated elements in a scammer's arsenal. It is now trivially easy to fabricate video testimonials, create convincing LinkedIn profiles, or populate review sites with coordinated, inauthentic feedback. The intelligent investor treats all testimonials as starting points for investigation, not endpoints of trust. Verification—through independent forums, multiple unconnected sources, and, if possible, direct communication with long-term users—is the only reliable way to transform anecdotal praise into genuine evidence.

A critical layer of protection lies in regulatory awareness. Even the most innovative platforms, if they interact with client funds or execute trades on their behalf, may fall under the purview of financial regulators. A provider that refuses to disclose its jurisdiction, licensing status, or compliance framework is effectively asking you to operate in a legal vacuum. The absence of regulation is not always proof of malfeasance—particularly in jurisdictions where certain software-only providers are not required to register—but it does shift the burden of risk entirely onto the user. Platforms operating legitimately within a regulatory framework will be transparent about their obligations and proactive in meeting them.

The challenge in spotting these red flags is that they often appear in combination, woven into marketing narratives that blend genuine capabilities with manufactured allure. This is why the most effective defence is not a checklist of specific warning signs but a cultivated mindset of sceptical curiosity. Trust is earned through clarity, verifiability, and demonstrated integrity over time. Any claim, feature, or selling point should be interrogated with the same question: "What evidence exists, independent of the provider's own marketing, to support this?"

The retail investor who internalises this approach not only avoids being drawn into fraudulent schemes but also becomes more adept at evaluating legitimate offerings. The discipline of demanding clear, verifiable, and proportionate claims naturally filters out providers who rely on exaggeration, opacity, and psychological pressure. It is not merely about avoiding being scammed; it is about *raising the standard of proof for everything you allow into your trading process.* In an industry where technology evolves rapidly but human vulnerabilities remain constant, the capacity to identify—and decisively walk away from—predatory marketing is as valuable as any algorithm you will ever deploy.

# Chapter 6
# From Theory to Market Test

There is a seductive danger in moving from spreadsheet to market, from theory to execution. The precision of a model, particularly one refined over years of historical data, can foster a false sense of inevitability. Numbers on a screen seem authoritative; backtested equity curves climb neatly from left to right, encouraging belief in a destiny of compounding success. Yet markets are not spreadsheets. They breathe, they evolve, and even the most elegant code can be punished if it has not been tested under conditions resembling reality. The passage from theory to live trading is where an algorithm leaves the controlled confines of its creator's design and confronts the unpredictability of the real world—a crucible that has humbled even the most sophisticated quants. Profitability is not born of theory alone; it is forged through the disciplined, sceptical, and iterative proving of that theory against the noise, frictions, and randomness inherent in markets.

Discipline begins with restraint. Paper trading—simulated trades executed without risking capital—is not a mark of timidity, but of professionalism. It is the financial analogue of a wind-tunnel test in aerospace: principles are validated before a pilot is ever strapped in. Too many retail traders skip this stage, eager to "see what happens" with real money, only to discover that a flawless backtest was a mirage—an artefact of curve-fitting, data leakage, or overoptimistic execution assumptions. The simulation stage is where fantasy meets operational friction: slippage, latency, data interruptions, and the subtle biases that creep in when theory meets reality. Done correctly, paper trading is not a box to tick but a structured, measurable process that either strengthens confidence in the model or saves one from costly disillusionment.

Testing without knowing what to measure is as futile as steering without a dashboard. Profit and loss alone offers a dangerously narrow perspective, particularly early on. A strategy can generate short-term gains while harbouring structural weaknesses—excessive drawdowns, erratic win/loss ratios, or dependence on rare market conditions—that erode capital over time. Key performance metrics such as maximum drawdown, Sharpe ratio, profit factor, and trade frequency are not academic exercises; they are early warning indicators, signalling whether a strategy is robust or merely fortunate. Focusing solely on net returns in initial tests is akin to judging a vessel's seaworthiness by its speed in calm waters. Storms come, and metrics should reveal whether the hull can endure.

First results are, more often than not, humbling. Even strategies that survive rigorous backtesting can reveal quirks in live-simulated performance: delayed entries, unexpected correlations with market events, or sensitivity to liquidity changes. This is not failure; it is diagnosis. The intelligent trader interprets early underperformance as information, not insult. The aim is not to confirm brilliance but to expose flaws—technical, structural, or behavioural—before real capital is at stake. Detachment is crucial. Every disappointing trade becomes a data point; every divergence from expected performance offers a clue about where reality departs from theory. Those lacking this detachment are prone to the classic error in early testing: abandoning a strategy after a single loss—or, equally perilous, doubling down after a single win.

Iteration, executed with precision, bridges flawed first drafts and sustainable trading models. Here, theory confronts empirical reality: it adapts or dies. Yet iteration is not tinkering for its own sake. Adjusting in response to every winning or losing trade—"chasing the last tick," as traders put it—breeds chaos rather than improvement. True iteration identifies patterns across statistically significant samples, isolates probable causes of deviation, and tests changes in controlled increments. It is disciplined experimentation, not reactive improvisation. The objective is not short-term perfection, but resilience over time.

Ego, in this phase, can be either ally or saboteur. Creators often grow attached to their code, reluctant to abandon a favourite indicator or parameter. Markets, however, are indifferent to attachment. Iteration demands repeated willingness to be wrong, in service of eventual rightness. It requires separating identity from outcome: seeing oneself not as the genius behind the code, but as an investigator ruthlessly interrogating it.

The path from theory to market test is not linear but cyclical—test, measure, interpret, refine, repeat. Those who view it as a single hurdle are most likely to falter when volatility returns, correlations break, or market regimes shift. Those who embrace it as an ongoing discipline are the ones whose strategies endure storms rather than merely exploiting calm seas. The goal is not simply to trade, but to trade in a way proven to withstand the world beyond the spreadsheet. By the time real capital is committed, the strategy should have faced every conceivable stress test—and a few surprises you could not foresee. This is the quiet, unglamorous work that separates professionals from hopefuls, and the profitable from the broken.

### Paper Trading for Proof

The temptation to skip straight to live trading is one of the most consistent and costly errors in the journey from algorithm design to execution. The argument is usually rationalised by impatience—"I'll just start small and see what happens"—but this overlooks a fundamental truth: *the market is designed to punish the untested.* Paper trading is not a bureaucratic hoop to jump through; it is a critical stage where the gap between an algorithm's theoretical promise and its real-world performance is exposed under safe conditions. In aviation, no aircraft goes directly from design sketches to passenger service. It first endures wind tunnel tests, simulator trials, and prototype flights without a commercial schedule to keep. Trading systems deserve the same respect for due process, because the financial equivalent of a crash is not repairable with spare parts and insurance payouts—it is capital permanently lost.

The first value of paper trading lies in its brutal confrontation with operational reality. Backtests are neat by nature; they run on perfect data, assume zero delay in execution, and never have to contend with the small irritations of market life—slippage, data feed errors, rejected orders, and network latency. These frictions, inconsequential in one or two trades, can quietly eat into profitability across hundreds. By running a strategy in a simulated live environment, you begin to quantify these hidden costs. You see how your algorithm behaves when the spread widens unexpectedly, or when a market order lags by a few seconds, or when price gaps past your stop level in illiquid conditions. This is not theory—it is the dress rehearsal where every snag is identified before the curtain rises.

Critics sometimes dismiss paper trading as meaningless because "you don't feel the psychology of real money." That criticism is half-right and entirely beside the point. Paper trading is not designed to replicate the emotional heat of live risk; it is designed to verify that your system works mechanically and statistically under conditions that mimic the real world. If you cannot achieve operational consistency without money on the line, you will not achieve it with money on the line. The goal at this stage is not to test your courage but to stress-test your code, your data pipeline, your execution assumptions, and your understanding of the market conditions in which the strategy is meant to thrive.

The second core benefit is the discipline of measurement. Paper trading without clear performance metrics is little more than fantasy role-play. This stage must be governed by the same statistical scrutiny you would apply to a backtest. The temptation is to focus on short-term profitability alone, but that blinds you to deeper structural insights. You should be tracking maximum drawdown, win rate, average win/loss ratio, exposure time, volatility of returns, and—crucially—how closely the live-simulated performance tracks the expectations set by your historical testing. Discrepancies between the two are diagnostic signals. They may reveal that your backtest overfitted to historical quirks, that your execution logic under real-time data is misaligned, or that market conditions have shifted in a way your system cannot currently accommodate.

Paper trading also acts as an intellectual safeguard against overconfidence. Developers are often enamoured with their models, particularly when they have invested months refining them. The simulated environment forces humility by exposing flaws that are invisible in theory. An algorithm that looked resilient over a decade of historical data may suddenly reveal its dependency on a specific volatility regime or its sensitivity to transaction costs. This is not a setback—it is a gift. Discovering these weaknesses in paper trading costs you nothing but time, while discovering them in live trading costs you capital, credibility, and often the patience to keep going.

The challenge is resisting the urge to cut this phase short. Many traders abandon paper testing as soon as they see a few weeks of profit, mistaking early success for structural soundness. In reality, the purpose of this stage is to accumulate *enough* data to draw statistically meaningful conclusions, which often means months of continuous testing across varying market conditions. A system that performs in trending markets but collapses in consolidation is not flawed per se—it is specialised. Knowing this before you go live allows you to make informed decisions about when to deploy capital and when to stand down. Without this insight, you risk stumbling into conditions your system was never designed to handle, attributing losses to "bad luck" instead of predictable incompatibility.

Done well, paper trading is not passive observation but active refinement. Each discrepancy between expected and actual outcomes should trigger investigation: Is the slippage consistent with your model's assumption? Are trade signals arriving as coded, or is data latency introducing noise? Are position sizes executing correctly, or is rounding affecting exposure? Every detail matters because markets are hostile to approximation. The paper stage is where you prove not only that your idea works in principle but that your infrastructure is robust enough to execute it faithfully under live conditions.

The professional mindset treats paper trading as the first true proof of concept, not a hurdle to be endured. The casual trader sees it as optional, which is why the casual trader's journey often ends with capital erosion rather than capital growth. The market offers no penalty for patience and no reward for haste. Every serious trader who has survived multiple market cycles can point to a period of rigorous simulation as the reason they avoided catastrophic early losses. The amateurs, by contrast, often describe their first live trades as "testing" the system—testing it with real money, real risk, and real consequences they were not prepared to bear.

Paper trading is not about building confidence; it is about earning it. It is where the discipline of quant finance meets the pragmatism of risk management. If your algorithm can survive the quiet, controlled trial of simulated execution—with all its frictions, imperfections, and operational demands—then, and only then, does it deserve to meet the unpredictable theatre of the live market. The alternative is gambling disguised as innovation, and the market has no shortage of stories about how that ends.

### Metrics That Matter

The most seductive number in trading is also the most misleading: percentage return. It commands attention, fuels marketing copy, and flatters the ego. Yet, for anyone serious about building a sustainable algorithmic strategy, raw returns are almost meaningless without context. *It is not what you make that determines survival, but what you risk, how consistently you perform, and how resilient your system is under stress.* The history of markets is littered with strategies that posted spectacular short-term gains only to collapse when volatility shifted, liquidity dried up, or a statistical blind spot was exposed. The difference between fleeting success and durable profitability lies in measuring the right things—metrics that diagnose the health of a system, not just its headline appeal.

A first principle for evaluating sustainability is risk-adjusted return. Two strategies may both deliver 20% in a year, but if one did so with violent swings in equity and the other with steady, controlled gains, they are not equivalent. The Sharpe ratio—though imperfect—remains one of the most widely used indicators here, as it captures excess return per unit of volatility. A low Sharpe ratio tells you that profits were more a product of luck or high-risk exposure than of robust, repeatable edge. However, the Sharpe ratio can be distorted when returns are not normally distributed, making the Sortino ratio a valuable complement, as it focuses only on downside volatility. The core insight is that *returns without a measure of variability are vanity statistics*. If you cannot survive the journey to those returns, the destination is irrelevant.

Drawdown metrics are equally essential and far more sobering. Maximum drawdown—measuring the steepest peak-to-trough equity decline—offers a clear picture of potential psychological and financial pain. It is easy to underestimate this metric when running backtests, but in live trading, a 40% drawdown can force even disciplined operators to abandon a system prematurely, locking in losses. The depth and duration of drawdowns reveal more about a strategy's true temperament than months of smooth performance. A system that takes years to recover from a drawdown may be mathematically viable but operationally untenable for most investors. This is where metrics cross into human factors: sustainability is not just a question of capital endurance but of psychological endurance.

Consistency of returns matters more than occasional bursts of brilliance. Monthly or weekly win rates, when examined over time, can expose patterns of dependency on specific market conditions. A strategy that wins 80% of the time in trending markets but collapses in choppy conditions is not inherently flawed, but its deployment must be conditional.

Too often, traders chase average returns without mapping the distribution of those returns, missing the opportunity to identify environmental dependencies. Equity curve stability—whether the performance line rises with manageable fluctuations or resembles a seismograph—offers a visual shorthand for this consistency, but it must be backed by statistical measures such as standard deviation of returns and rolling Sharpe ratios over multiple timeframes.

Trade-level analysis brings another layer of insight. Average win size versus average loss size (the profit factor) indicates whether the system's edge comes from many small wins or fewer large ones. Both models can be profitable, but their vulnerability to variance differs. A strategy reliant on a small number of outsized winners is more exposed to streaks of unfavourable conditions than one that compounds smaller, consistent gains. Coupled with this is expectancy—the average amount you can expect to win or lose per trade over the long term. Expectancy strips away the noise of individual trades and focuses attention on whether the statistical underpinnings of the system are genuinely in your favour.

Transaction cost sensitivity is one of the most overlooked sustainability metrics. A backtest that ignores realistic commission and slippage assumptions can transform a seemingly profitable system into a loss-making one in live conditions. This is especially relevant for high-frequency or short-hold strategies, where even fractional increases in execution costs can erode profitability. Testing a strategy's break-even point in terms of costs—how much additional slippage or spread widening it can absorb before turning unprofitable—provides a vital durability check. It is a reminder that sustainability is not just about surviving market volatility, but about enduring the quieter, cumulative toll of micro-costs.

Capacity and scalability must also be quantified, not assumed. A strategy that thrives on small capital allocations can falter when scaled, as its trades begin to influence market prices or liquidity becomes insufficient to absorb larger orders without impact. This is particularly relevant in niche or low-volume markets where apparent profitability in paper testing does not translate to real-world execution. Tracking fill rates and average market depth during simulated scaling tests can prevent the mistake of overestimating a strategy's growth potential. Sustainability is as much about matching your strategy to the liquidity environment as it is about statistical robustness.

Correlation to other strategies or market indices is another subtle but powerful measure. A system that produces excellent standalone returns but is highly correlated to equity markets may offer little diversification benefit and be vulnerable to the same systemic shocks. Understanding correlation allows you to position a strategy within a portfolio in a way that truly diversifies risk, rather than duplicating exposure under a different name. This is where sustainability transcends the individual system—it is about how it contributes to the stability of the whole.

Finally, adaptability metrics—though harder to quantify—may be the truest predictors of long-term survival. Markets evolve, and a system rigidly optimised for past conditions is inherently fragile. Tracking how performance shifts under different volatility regimes, interest rate environments, or sector rotations can help you identify whether your strategy's edge is timeless or transient. Adaptive robustness tests—intentionally stressing the system with data outside its design parameters—are invaluable here. Sustainability is not about perfection in a fixed environment but resilience in a shifting one.

The discipline of focusing on these metrics forces you to confront the uncomfortable: the limits of your strategy, the conditions it cannot handle, the fragility that hides behind appealing returns. A strategy that scores modestly on headline profitability but strongly on these sustainability measures is more likely to survive the test of time than one with dazzling returns and glaring weaknesses in risk control, capacity, or adaptability. The market's ultimate filter is not generosity but attrition, and the traders who remain standing are those who measure what truly matters, long after the noise of initial performance has faded.

### Interpreting Your First Results

The first set of results from a freshly deployed algorithm—whether in paper trading or with limited capital—often provokes an emotional reaction that clouds judgment. A winning streak can create a false sense of mastery; a losing streak can trigger doubts about the strategy's validity or the trader's competence. Yet these early numbers, stripped of emotional colouring, are neither a final verdict nor a trivial curiosity. *They are a window into the practical realities of your system's behaviour, revealing not just whether it made or lost money, but how it interacts with market conditions, execution constraints, and your own decision-making framework.* The key is to approach them not as a scorecard, but as a diagnostic report.

One of the first interpretative errors to avoid is overweighing outcome over process. If your strategy happened to launch during an unusually favourable market phase, strong early returns may conceal fragility. Likewise, a poor start might simply be the result of deploying during adverse conditions the system was not optimised for. The objective is to decouple performance from context—overlaying your trades with contemporaneous market data to see whether outcomes were the result of edge, luck, or avoidable error. For instance, if a momentum algorithm launched during a week of choppy, range-bound trading underperformed, that is not inherently a flaw; it may simply validate the need for conditional deployment filters.

Equally important is to look beyond aggregate profit and loss and examine the structure of returns. Were winning trades concentrated in one or two outsized positions, or did they emerge consistently across many small gains? Were losses controlled and consistent with your risk model, or did one rogue trade breach expected parameters? This distinction matters because a strategy with a smooth distribution of returns tends to be more sustainable, whereas one dependent on infrequent large wins is more vulnerable to variance. It is also here that you uncover whether your trade sizing logic holds up in practice—whether you are inadvertently concentrating risk in ways your backtest failed to reveal.

Execution quality is another layer often ignored in first-result analysis. Live or simulated trading introduces frictions absent from backtesting: slippage, partial fills, delayed order routing, and fluctuating spreads. A system may appear to underperform not because its logic is unsound, but because operational realities erode its theoretical edge. This is where measuring "implementation shortfall"—the gap between the price your algorithm intended to transact at and the price actually achieved—becomes invaluable. If your strategy is sound but suffers from persistent execution drag, you are dealing with an operational, not strategic, problem—one that can be solved through broker selection, order type refinement, or timing adjustments.

Comparing actual drawdowns to projected drawdowns from your test data is a critical stress test of your risk assumptions. If your first live drawdown is significantly deeper or faster than your backtest predicted, it could mean your risk model underestimates market volatility or fails to account for clustering of adverse events. Conversely, if your drawdowns are shallower than expected, it may indicate you have capacity to increase position sizing or take more simultaneous trades without breaching comfort thresholds. Either outcome provides actionable intelligence—what matters is your willingness to interrogate it without bias.

One of the subtler insights from early performance lies in regime sensitivity. By mapping your results against volatility indices, interest rate changes, earnings seasons, or geopolitical events, you can begin to identify the environmental conditions under which your strategy thrives or falters. This pattern-matching should not lead to knee-jerk optimisation—overfitting to a small sample is one of the fastest paths to ruin—but it can inform a longer-term plan for conditional activation. A mean-reversion system that consistently struggles during high-volatility spikes is not necessarily flawed; it may simply be designed for calmer waters, and recognising this early allows you to protect it from hostile regimes.

It is also essential to assess whether your psychological execution matched the system's intent. Even in paper trading, human interference can creep in—hesitating to take a signal, overriding an entry, or exiting early "just in case." If your first results deviate meaningfully from what the strategy would have done without intervention, your analysis must separate the algorithm's true performance from the trader's behavioural imprint. This is where the first results are as much a test of personal discipline as of system design; you may discover that a technically sound strategy fails in practice because its drawdowns or signal frequency clash with your temperament.

Early data should also be used to validate—or challenge—your performance metrics hierarchy. Before going live, most traders select a small set of key indicators to track: Sharpe or Sortino ratios, maximum drawdown, win rate, profit factor, average trade duration. The first results provide a chance to see whether those metrics are telling you something useful. You may find, for instance, that your win rate is high but your profit factor is mediocre, suggesting that while the system wins often, it does not win big enough to offset its occasional losses. Conversely, a low win rate paired with a strong profit factor could indicate a system that thrives on rare but large moves—a profile that demands psychological resilience but can be very profitable if understood correctly.

Perhaps the most difficult discipline in interpreting early results is resisting premature optimisation. It is tempting to tinker after a handful of trades, adjusting parameters to "fix" what appears broken. But statistical noise is a formidable deceiver; changing a system in response to a small, unrepresentative sample is often the beginning of a destructive cycle of overfitting. A more disciplined approach is to log all perceived weaknesses, hypotheses, and improvement ideas, but defer material changes until you have sufficient data to justify them. The threshold for "sufficient" will vary by system, but as a rule, the smaller the edge and the more volatile the returns, the larger your data sample must be before drawing conclusions.

In the end, the first set of results is best seen as reconnaissance, not judgment. It is your initial opportunity to see the terrain of live or simulated trading—the potholes, the unexpected slopes, the moments when theory collides with reality. Even disappointing results can be valuable if they reveal mismatches between design assumptions and market behaviour, highlight operational weaknesses, or expose psychological stress points. The traders who survive and thrive are those who approach these early signals with clinical detachment, harvesting insights without overreacting, and letting the data—not their emotions—set the course for refinement. The real measure of a trader at this stage is not the balance of wins and losses, but the quality of the questions they begin to ask.

## Iterating Intelligently

The temptation to make sweeping adjustments after every trade—particularly a losing one—is among the most insidious threats to any algorithmic trading strategy. It is a behaviour rooted in the deeply human desire to regain control in the face of uncertainty, and in markets, uncertainty is the default state. But while reactive tinkering can provide the illusion of progress, it more often destroys the very statistical edge the system was designed to exploit. *The discipline of intelligent iteration lies in separating the signal from the noise, in learning to identify when changes are justified by evidence rather than provoked by emotion.*

At its core, iteration is a process of hypothesis testing. Each adjustment to a model—whether to its parameters, execution logic, or risk management rules—represents a bet that the change will improve long-term performance. This means that a single trade, or even a short cluster of trades, is almost never a sufficient dataset on which to base a change. Statistical variance ensures that even the most robust strategies will endure losing streaks that appear alarming in the moment but are entirely consistent with long-term profitability. The disciplined practitioner accepts these fluctuations as a cost of doing business and refrains from "chasing" the last outcome, however tempting.

One effective way to enforce discipline is to set predefined review intervals—moments when you will examine your strategy's performance holistically, independent of recent results. For example, you might conduct a full diagnostic every 250 trades or at the end of each quarter, whichever comes first. This creates a buffer between stimulus and response, preventing knee-jerk alterations that could inadvertently break a functioning system. At these intervals, you can assess performance across varied market conditions, compare live results to your backtest expectations, and identify whether underperformance stems from random variation, market regime change, or a genuine flaw in the system's design.

The danger of ad hoc iteration is not merely the loss of a statistical edge—it is the erosion of methodological integrity. When changes are made without sufficient data, you introduce survivorship bias into your process. You end up with a model that has been repeatedly fitted to the idiosyncrasies of small, unrepresentative market samples, producing an illusion of optimisation that collapses under broader testing. This is how traders drift from robust, conceptually sound strategies into fragile, overfitted systems that fail catastrophically in live conditions.

Intelligent iteration requires a clear framework for deciding when a modification is warranted. The first step is to define, in advance, what constitutes statistically significant underperformance. For instance, if your backtest suggests a maximum historical drawdown of 12% with a standard deviation of 3%, you might stipulate that a live drawdown exceeding 18% is grounds for deeper investigation. Similarly, you could establish thresholds for key metrics such as win rate, profit factor, or average trade duration, with deviation beyond these limits triggering a structured review. The point is to let pre-set rules—not transient emotions—determine when iteration occurs.

When a change is justified, the adjustment should be narrow, precise, and testable. A common mistake is to overhaul multiple components at once—altering entry criteria, stop-loss placement, and position sizing simultaneously—making it impossible to attribute any improvement or decline to a specific change. Instead, modify a single variable, document your reasoning, and track th[illegible]utcomes in isolation. This scientific approach [illegible]rity of cause and effect, allowing you to build [illegible]derstanding of your system's sensitivities rather than stumbling blindly from one configuration to another.

It is equally important to distinguish between structural and cyclical underperformance. Structural issues arise from flaws in the strategy's design—perhaps it relies on indicators that lag too heavily in volatile markets, or it ignores transaction costs in a way that erodes profitability. Cyclical underperformance, on the other hand, is a natural consequence of the strategy's market dependency; a trend-following model will inevitably struggle in range-bound conditions, just as mean-reversion systems suffer during runaway moves. The former demands re-engineering; the latter demands patience, discipline, and perhaps a framework for selectively pausing or hedging the strategy in hostile environments. Misdiagnosing the cause leads to unnecessary changes that degrade performance rather than improve it.

Real-world examples illustrate the stakes. Consider a proprietary desk running a high-frequency strategy optimised for tight spreads in liquid currency pairs. A sudden widening of spreads due to central bank policy shifts reduced the strategy's hit rate for several weeks. An inexperienced team might have rewritten the entry logic entirely; the seasoned team instead verified that the underperformance was regime-driven, not structural, and temporarily reduced position size until spreads normalised. The result was preservation of the original edge without unnecessary code changes that could have invalidated years of testing.

Iteration also demands an awareness of your own behavioural biases. Loss aversion—the psychological tendency to weigh losses more heavily than gains—can lead to abandoning a profitable system after a perfectly ordinary drawdown. Recency bias encourages overweighting the last few trades, particularly if they were emotionally charged. Intelligent iteration requires constant vigilance against these biases, and one way to counter them is to maintain a detailed performance log that contextualises recent results within the system's historical norms. When you can see that the last three losses are statistically indistinguishable from similar sequences in the backtest, the urge to intervene prematurely diminishes.

Finally, intelligent iteration is as much about what you do not change as what you do. The stability of a trading system is an asset in itself, allowing you to accumulate enough data to make statistically sound decisions. Frequent alterations, no matter how well-intentioned, disrupt this stability and can mask whether the system was working in the first place. The trader who learns to wait—who can endure the discomfort of inaction while collecting evidence—ultimately commands a deeper understanding of their system's true nature and potential.

In markets, iteration is inevitable. Conditions shift, liquidity fluctuates, and the behaviour of participants evolves. The question is not whether you will adjust, but how. To iterate intelligently is to commit to a standard of evidence, to resist the lure of impulsive fixes, and to cultivate the patience necessary for meaningful learning. It is this discipline—not the number of lines of code you modify—that separates a mature, data-driven practitioner from one who is simply chasing the ghost of the last trade.

# Chapter 7
# Guardrails for Real Money

Deploying real capital transforms the theoretical elegance of algorithmic trading into a high-stakes experiment where every oversight, flaw, or latent bias carries financial consequence. Backtests may have been meticulous, paper trading may have instilled confidence, yet the moment real money enters the arena, the demands—both psychological and structural—shift sharply. In the unforgiving reality of markets, the question ceases to be merely whether a strategy works; it becomes whether it can survive. Guardrails—those pre-engineered constraints designed to prevent a system from spiralling into ruin—are not optional features of professional trading; they are the invisible scaffolding that allows risk-taking to remain both sustainable and scalable. Paradoxically, these safeguards, which might at first glance appear constraining, are precisely what grant a trader freedom: the freedom to let a system operate without constant intervention, the freedom to absorb inevitable losses without catastrophe, and the freedom to focus on refinement rather than damage control.

Position sizing is the first, and perhaps most immediate, of these guardrails—a domain where algorithms excel at enforcing discipline. Humans are notoriously inconsistent in allocation, often inflating trade sizes after a string of wins or shrinking them in the wake of losses, undermining recovery. Hard-coded rules—whether fixed fractional, volatility-adjusted, or value-at-risk-based—strip mood and momentum from the equation. These rules do more than limit exposure; they establish a consistent risk profile that renders performance data interpretable. Without them, every adjustment in size becomes another variable muddying the signal of a strategy's effectiveness. A system that wins spectacularly one week only to give it all back the next is not merely volatile—it is structurally unstable.

Stop losses and exit signals, frequently dismissed as simple "safety switches," are in truth the execution layer of risk philosophy. A poorly designed exit either truncates winners or allows losers to metastasise. Traditional stop losses—fixed percentages or monetary thresholds—are straightforward but often too blunt for algorithmic nuance. More sophisticated designs integrate volatility bands, trailing logic, or adaptive thresholds responsive to real-time market behaviour. Exits demand the same analytical rigor as entries. A strategy that wins 60 per cent of its trades but lacks disciplined exits will inevitably face a single trade capable of erasing months of gains. Intelligent exit logic does not merely apply the brakes; it actively guards the portfolio, closing positions when the statistical odds shift materially against them.

Guardrails must operate not only at the trade level but across the portfolio. Diversification—purposeful rather than haphazard—is a structural defence against concentration risk. This is not the lazy approach of scattering capital across dozens of assets without rationale. True diversification entails curating strategies with uncorrelated performance drivers: a mean-reversion equity model alongside a trend-following commodity system; an intraday volatility play offset by a long-term macro thesis. The aim is to ensure no single strategy or market condition dominates the portfolio's risk profile. If volatility spikes obliterate the entire portfolio, it is not diversification—it is a single bet in disguise. Algorithms can enforce this mechanically, capping capital allocation to any one strategy or sector and dynamically rebalancing as correlations evolve.

Perhaps the most overlooked form of risk management is the automation of the safety net itself. Many traders treat risk controls as guidelines, applied manually and subject to emotional judgment. The result is predictable: when stress runs high, guidelines bend. By embedding these controls directly into the algorithm—maximum drawdown limits that halt trading for the day, real-time margin checks preventing over-leverage, circuit breakers that liquidate positions during extreme events—you create a protective layer impervious to hesitation or second-guessing. This automation does not obviate human oversight; it ensures that the first line of defence is steadfast, even when the human is distracted, fatigued, or emotionally compromised.

The danger lies in treating guardrails as afterthoughts—tacked on late rather than woven into the system's architecture from inception. In reality, they must be embedded from the first line of code and tested with the same rigour as any trading logic. A system that is profitable but fragile is a time bomb; a system moderately profitable but robust can scale, endure shocks, and evolve. Rising markets may conceal this distinction, but it becomes brutally clear during regime shifts, liquidity crises, or unexpected geopolitical events. When such moments arrive, there is no opportunity to design new safeguards; they must already be battle-tested and trusted.

Trading without guardrails is akin to piloting a high-performance car at full speed without brakes or seat belts—not reckless out of bravado, but reckless because the consequences of unpredictability are accepted as inevitable. Markets do not reward absence of control with higher returns; they punish it with losses that compound faster than they can be recouped. Professionals understand that profitability is meaningful only when paired with survivability. The art of trading lies not in maximising gains under ideal conditions, but in ensuring the system endures when conditions deteriorate. This chapter examines the structures, principles, and implementations that transform raw strategies into resilient market participants—frameworks that turn volatility from threat into manageable variable, and risk from uncontrolled hazard into deliberate, quantifiable choice. By its conclusion, the reader will understand not only which guardrails to install but how to embed them into the algorithm's very DNA, ensuring that when real capital is at stake, the system trades with both ambition and resilience.

## Position Sizing Rules: Demonstrates how algorithms can enforce disciplined allocation and prevent overexposure

The most dangerous misconception in trading is that profitability is dictated solely by finding the right entry and exit points. In reality, even a brilliant strategy can be rendered unprofitable—or outright destructive—by reckless allocation. Position sizing is not merely a secondary parameter; it is the structural skeleton of capital management. Without it, the trader is like a skilled pilot flying without any knowledge of fuel consumption—perhaps soaring at times, but one miscalculation away from running out of resources entirely. The difference between a system that survives market turbulence and one that collapses often lies not in predictive accuracy but in the disciplined enforcement of how much capital is put at risk at any given moment. Algorithms, unlike human operators, do not suffer from adrenaline-induced overconfidence or fear-driven hesitation. They can execute position sizing rules with unwavering consistency, ensuring that no single trade has the potential to sink the entire account. The irony is that while human traders frequently focus on maximising gains, seasoned professionals know that limiting losses—through prudent sizing—is the more reliable path to compounding returns over time.

At its core, position sizing is about controlling risk exposure relative to the size of the trading account and the volatility of the market or asset in question. A fixed-percentage model—risking, for instance, 1% or 2% of account equity per trade—offers a straightforward discipline: losses scale down as the account shrinks, and gains scale up as it grows. While simple, this method protects against catastrophic drawdowns and forces a trader to think in relative rather than absolute terms. In practice, however, the simplicity of fixed percentage sizing can be misleading. If the underlying asset's volatility is not accounted for, two trades risking the same percentage may in reality expose the trader to vastly different levels of market fluctuation. This is where volatility-adjusted sizing becomes more precise, using metrics such as Average True Range (ATR) or standard deviation to dynamically adjust position sizes so that each trade carries a consistent dollar-value risk, regardless of market conditions.

Consider the case of two traders running the same equity strategy—one risking a fixed monetary amount per trade, the other adjusting risk according to volatility. When market conditions shift abruptly, producing wider price swings, the fixed-dollar trader is likely to experience disproportionately large losses, as the same nominal exposure now entails greater variability. The volatility-adjusted trader, however, automatically scales down position sizes during high-volatility periods, cushioning the impact of unfavourable moves. Over a large enough data set, the latter's equity curve will typically show smaller drawdowns, steadier growth, and less variance in returns—critical qualities for long-term sustainability. This demonstrates why *discipline in sizing is as important as accuracy in signals*.

Yet position sizing is not only about defensive capital preservation; it also influences opportunity capture. Kelly Criterion, a mathematically derived formula used widely in gambling and later adapted to trading, offers a theoretical model for optimal bet sizing to maximise geometric account growth. While alluring in its precision, the Kelly approach assumes perfect knowledge of win probability and payoff ratio—conditions rarely met in live markets. Moreover, pure Kelly sizing is highly aggressive, often producing intolerable volatility in account value. Many professional traders, aware of these risks, employ a fractional Kelly approach, using perhaps half or a quarter of the theoretically optimal size to balance growth potential with emotional and financial stability. The broader lesson is that theoretical optimality must be tempered by the real-world constraints of uncertainty and capital preservation.

The human element in position sizing failures is difficult to overstate. Traders without enforced allocation rules tend to increase size after wins (believing they are "on a streak") and either reduce size or overcompensate after losses (seeking to avoid pain or recover quickly). This oscillation destroys the statistical reliability of performance data and introduces emotional volatility into the decision-making process. Algorithms can neutralise this by embedding sizing logic directly into the execution layer, ensuring that *every trade adheres to the pre-defined framework regardless of recent performance*. By automating allocation, you eliminate not only impulsive oversizing after a winning streak but also the subtle erosion of returns caused by trading too small after a temporary setback.

One underappreciated benefit of algorithmic enforcement is that it enables systematic scaling—adjusting trade sizes not based on recent emotions but on structural triggers such as equity milestones, volatility regimes, or changes in correlation within a portfolio. For example, an algorithm might reduce aggregate exposure if correlations between assets spike, signalling a higher systemic risk environment. Conversely, it might increase size in low-volatility conditions where the risk-adjusted reward is more favourable. These scaling adjustments can be designed to operate invisibly in the background, protecting the trader from unconscious concentration risk.

Case studies from professional funds illustrate how crucial disciplined sizing can be. During the volatility shock of early 2018, many discretionary traders suffered rapid losses as equity index volatility spiked and price swings widened beyond normal expectations. Funds with algorithms that dynamically reduced position sizes in response to volatility, however, not only preserved capital but were able to redeploy at larger sizes once conditions stabilised, effectively turning risk control into an offensive advantage. Similarly, in the currency markets, models that limit per-trade exposure relative to both account equity and daily range have shown resilience against flash crashes that wiped out traders with static, oversized positions.

Position sizing rules also have a philosophical dimension that speaks to the deeper purpose of systematic trading. By defining risk before a trade is taken, you acknowledge that uncertainty is not an occasional hazard but the fundamental condition of markets. This reframes the trader's role from "predicting outcomes" to "managing probabilities," a shift that tends to produce steadier decision-making and more consistent returns. Over time, this approach fosters an operational resilience that outlasts any single strategy or market cycle. A trader who survives can adapt; one who blows up cannot.

The ultimate sophistication in position sizing is achieved when algorithms integrate multiple layers of discipline—risk-per-trade caps, volatility adjustments, portfolio-level exposure limits, and dynamic scaling—into a coherent whole. Each layer serves as a failsafe for the others, creating redundancy in the risk management system. Such layered design ensures that even if one measure fails—say, volatility remains artificially low before a sudden spike—the others still mitigate the potential damage. The goal is not to eliminate risk entirely, which is neither possible nor profitable, but to calibrate it so that no single trade or sequence of trades can irreversibly damage the capital base.

In professional trading, position sizing rules are not afterthoughts; they are the foundation upon which the rest of the strategy is built. They dictate not just how much you can gain but, more critically, how much you are allowed to lose. By allowing algorithms to enforce these rules mechanically, you remove the weakest link in the chain—the human tendency to rationalise exceptions in the heat of the moment. The disciplined allocation they produce is not restrictive but liberating: it allows strategies to be executed with confidence, performance to be measured with clarity, and capital to be preserved for the trades that matter most. In the end, the trader who masters position sizing is not playing for the next win but for the next thousand trades, and that is the mindset from which lasting success is built.

### Stop Losses and Exit Signals: Covers both traditional and algorithm-enhanced exit strategies

The hardest decision in trading is rarely when to enter—it is when to get out. Entry points can be engineered with precision and tested endlessly in simulations, but exits confront the trader with the reality of imperfect foresight. They demand an acceptance of loss, an abandonment of the seductive "maybe it will turn around" thought, and an ability to act without hesitation when a strategy dictates. Poor exit discipline has destroyed more trading accounts than poor entries ever have. It is the domain where hope and regret most effectively undermine rational decision-making. For this reason, professional trading operations—both discretionary and algorithmic—treat stop losses and exit signals not as tactical conveniences but as structural safeguards.

A stop loss, at its simplest, is a pre-set price level at which a position will be closed to prevent further loss. This mechanical principle is as old as modern markets, yet its execution can vary dramatically. The most basic approach is a fixed-price stop, defined at the moment of trade initiation and left unchanged. While simple to implement, fixed stops ignore market volatility, making them prone to either premature triggering during normal price noise or dangerously slow activation during high-volatility events. More adaptive models use *volatility-based stops,* often calculated via the Average True Range (ATR), so that the distance to the stop dynamically expands or contracts in relation to prevailing market conditions. Such stops maintain proportionality: in calmer markets, they remain tighter to protect capital; in turbulent markets, they allow room for the strategy to operate without constant false exits.

Algorithmic enhancements elevate stop loss logic beyond fixed parameters. An algorithm can continuously assess multiple variables—volatility, liquidity depth, intraday momentum shifts—and adjust stops in real time. This means a position in a highly liquid currency pair during stable market conditions might have a tight protective band, while the same nominal risk in a thinly traded commodity futures contract would require more breathing space. Beyond price and volatility, AI-driven systems can integrate fundamental and sentiment data, tightening stops if, for instance, breaking news increases the probability of an adverse market move, even if price action has not yet reflected it. This anticipatory adjustment is something manual traders struggle to execute consistently, given the sheer speed of information flow.

Trailing stops represent another evolution of the exit discipline, designed to lock in profits while still allowing for further gains. A *static trailing stop* moves only in the direction of the trade, maintaining a set distance from the highest favourable price achieved since entry. This ensures that profits are never given back beyond a certain threshold. The more advanced *dynamic trailing stop* adjusts the trail distance itself based on market structure—such as recent swing lows in an uptrend—or statistical measures like volatility compression. By combining trailing logic with volatility sensitivity, algorithms can avoid the common trap of being stopped out during minor retracements, only to watch the market continue in the anticipated direction.

Yet stop losses alone do not define an exit strategy. In many cases, *exit signals* based on performance metrics, time decay, or a shift in trade validity provide more effective control. For example, a trend-following model might exit not because a price has crossed a predetermined loss threshold, but because its moving average slope has flattened beyond a certain tolerance, signalling that momentum has dissipated. A mean-reversion strategy might exit when a price returns to a statistically neutral range, even if the profit is modest, because the strategy's statistical edge vanishes beyond that point. Algorithms excel in executing these context-sensitive exits, where the decision to close is not reactive to loss alone but informed by the integrity of the trade setup itself.

Time-based exits are often overlooked but can be critical in preventing capital from stagnating in positions with diminishing prospects. A position that has not moved significantly in the intended direction within a defined holding period may be signalling that the underlying market condition has changed. Algorithmic time stops can be combined with price and volatility triggers to ensure that capital is always allocated where the statistical probabilities remain favourable. For instance, in high-frequency strategies, the difference between a 500-millisecond exit and a two-second hold can determine profitability over thousands of trades—a decision far too rapid for human intervention but trivial for an automated system.

One of the enduring debates among traders is whether tighter or looser stops produce better results. The tension lies between avoiding catastrophic losses and preventing the frequent small losses that erode capital and confidence. There is no universally correct answer—different strategies thrive under different stop philosophies. What is critical is that the chosen approach aligns with the underlying statistical profile of the strategy. A high win-rate, small-gain strategy can tolerate tighter stops, as the majority of trades close in profit and the small losses are quickly recovered. A low win-rate, high-reward trend strategy needs looser stops to survive the inevitable string of small losses before a large win arrives. Algorithms can test and optimise these trade-offs at a scale and speed beyond manual capability, but even they require human oversight to ensure that the optimisation does not lead to curve-fitting—a model that is perfect on paper but fragile in reality.

Importantly, stop losses and exit signals must be evaluated not in isolation but as part of the broader portfolio context. A single position might not appear dangerous in isolation, but if it shares high correlation with several other open trades, its potential loss could be amplified by market-wide moves. Algorithms can integrate correlation matrices into their stop logic, tightening or triggering exits when systemic risk rises. For example, during a market shock that simultaneously affects equities, currencies, and commodities, an AI system might cut correlated exposures aggressively, even if the individual positions have not yet hit their stop thresholds. This is a level of interlinked risk control that human traders often recognise too late.

The psychological benefit of algorithmic stop enforcement should not be underestimated. In discretionary trading, the temptation to "move the stop just a little further" is a persistent threat. This often stems from the cognitive bias known as *loss aversion*, where the pain of taking a realised loss outweighs the rational decision to preserve capital. By embedding stop logic in the execution code itself, algorithms remove the opportunity for mid-trade negotiation with oneself. This not only preserves discipline but also produces cleaner performance data, since every trade follows the same rules without subjective interference. That data integrity, in turn, strengthens the validity of subsequent optimisations and refinements.

Historical market events repeatedly validate the necessity of disciplined exits. During the Swiss franc shock of January 2015, when the Swiss National Bank unexpectedly abandoned its currency peg, forex markets moved too rapidly for manual stops to be executed at their intended prices. Traders who relied on basic broker-implemented stops without slippage control suffered heavy losses, in some cases wiping out entire accounts. Funds with algorithms that combined multiple exit signals—volatility triggers, correlation alerts, and dynamic stop recalculations—were not immune to losses, but many avoided catastrophic outcomes by acting milliseconds faster and reducing exposure before liquidity completely evaporated.

Ultimately, the sophistication of an exit strategy is measured not by how often it locks in the maximum possible profit, but by how reliably it prevents ruin while allowing a strategy's statistical edge to unfold. Stops that are too tight will choke off that edge; stops that are too loose will let losses spiral beyond recovery. Algorithms provide the precision, speed, and consistency to maintain that balance, free from the corrosive influence of hope and fear. By integrating both traditional protective measures and adaptive, data-driven enhancements, they transform stop losses and exit signals from blunt tools into finely tuned instruments—ones capable of safeguarding capital while letting profits run in alignment with a strategy's true potential.

## Diversification by Design: Shows how to structure portfolios so no single strategy dominates risk

In trading, survival is not merely about generating returns—it is about avoiding concentrations of risk that can undo years of compounding in a single misjudged moment. The seductive danger lies in success itself. A single strategy, perhaps a trend-following model in equities or a mean-reversion system in currency pairs, begins to deliver a consistent edge. Confidence grows, position sizes creep up, and before long, this single engine is pulling most of the portfolio's weight. This feels efficient—until market conditions shift and that engine stalls. The collapse is rarely gradual; it is sudden, and often terminal for traders who have allowed performance dependency to morph into risk dependency. *True diversification is not about holding multiple positions—it is about ensuring no one strategy, instrument, or market environment can dictate the fate of the entire portfolio.*

Many traders confuse diversification with variety. They may hold positions in ten different securities or run five distinct trading strategies, believing themselves well-hedged. But if those assets move in lockstep when volatility spikes, or if those strategies are all implicitly optimised for the same type of market behaviour, the diversity is illusory. During the 2008 financial crisis, portfolios that looked broad on paper collapsed because their supposedly independent holdings—bank stocks, real estate trusts, and corporate bonds—were all exposed to the same underlying systemic risk: credit contraction. In algorithmic trading, the equivalent mistake is running multiple models that all rely on trend persistence during low-volatility conditions. Such strategies will all falter, and often simultaneously, when volatility suddenly rises or trend structures break down.

Algorithmic portfolio design offers a structural advantage in managing this hidden correlation. Unlike discretionary traders, who may rely on intuition to sense when different strategies "feel" independent, algorithms can quantify dependencies precisely through correlation matrices, cointegration tests, and drawdown clustering analysis.

These tools allow the portfolio architect to detect when apparent diversification is masking deep interdependencies. For example, two strategies might be based on different asset classes—one on commodities, one on foreign exchange—but both may exploit the same momentum principle triggered by similar macroeconomic events. A well-designed algorithmic risk engine can detect this latent connection and limit the combined exposure, even if the positions appear unrelated on the surface.

The most robust portfolios are often constructed on multiple axes of diversification. The first is asset class: equities, bonds, commodities, currencies, and alternative markets such as cryptocurrencies. The second is strategy type: trend-following, mean reversion, statistical arbitrage, volatility harvesting, event-driven, and more. The third is time horizon: high-frequency, intraday, swing, and position trading. A trader who can blend these dimensions effectively reduces the likelihood that any single market phase will inflict broad, synchronised damage. Crucially, diversification is not a one-time design choice but a continuous process. Correlations are not fixed; they expand and contract with market regimes. An asset that behaved as a diversifier during one period can become a source of risk concentration in another. Gold, for instance, has alternated between acting as a safe-haven hedge and moving in tandem with equities, depending on inflation expectations and interest rate cycles. Algorithms can detect such regime shifts in real time and adjust allocations accordingly.

Position weighting is equally critical. Even if strategies are uncorrelated, over-allocating capital to the historically best-performing model can inadvertently make it a portfolio's single point of failure. The discipline lies in *allocating risk, not just capital*. This means normalising position sizes by volatility and expected drawdown rather than simply funding each strategy equally or by nominal returns. A high-volatility strategy with exceptional historical gains should command no more risk budget than a lower-volatility strategy with modest but stable returns. By calibrating exposure in this way, an algorithmic portfolio can preserve the statistical advantage of each strategy while preventing any single one from disproportionately influencing portfolio-level performance.

A telling case study is the approach taken by certain multi-strategy hedge funds that use *risk parity* principles. These funds allocate capital such that each strategy, or each asset class, contributes equally to total portfolio volatility. The result is that a historically volatile asset such as commodities receives a smaller nominal allocation, while a lower-volatility asset such as government bonds receives a larger one, balancing their overall impact on risk. This ensures that the portfolio's fate is not overly tied to any one segment, even if that segment has been historically more profitable. Algorithmic systems can extend this principle by recalculating these allocations daily or even intraday, based on updated volatility and correlation data.

Yet diversification is not without its trade-offs. By spreading capital across uncorrelated strategies, a trader inevitably dilutes the impact of their highest-conviction ideas. There is a philosophical tension here between maximising return potential and minimising blow-up risk. Over-diversification—sometimes called *diworsification*—can result in a portfolio that is so diluted that no edge meaningfully drives performance. This is particularly dangerous in algorithmic contexts, where each strategy must be robust enough to justify its capital allocation after accounting for execution costs, slippage, and maintenance overhead. The discipline lies in setting a high entry bar for inclusion in the portfolio, favouring a smaller set of truly independent, well-validated strategies over a larger set with superficial diversity.

Stress testing is the final and often underappreciated pillar of diversification by design. Historical backtests can reveal how a portfolio behaved during past crises, but *synthetic stress scenarios*—simulations of hypothetical but plausible market shocks—are essential to uncover vulnerabilities. For example, an algorithmic portfolio might be tested against a sudden liquidity freeze, a multi-day exchange outage, or a geopolitical event causing correlated sell-offs across asset classes. Such simulations often reveal that the real risk in a portfolio is not in its everyday volatility, but in the rare but inevitable periods when correlations spike towards one. By integrating these scenarios into the portfolio design process, algorithms can pre-emptively adjust allocations or embed defensive overlays to protect capital.

Perhaps the most profound advantage of algorithmic diversification is its ability to enforce discipline without human interference. Human traders often erode their own diversification by overweighting recent winners or abandoning lagging strategies too soon. Algorithms, by contrast, can maintain target allocations mechanically, rebalancing according to predefined rules regardless of recent performance swings. This insulates the portfolio from recency bias and the psychological urge to "bet bigger" on what just worked, which is precisely how concentration risk creeps in.

Diversification by design is therefore not simply a defensive posture; it is an architecture for longevity. Markets are adaptive systems—edges erode, correlations shift, and dominant strategies fade. A portfolio that survives these changes is one that assumes no single approach will work forever, and therefore distributes risk in a way that no single failure can dictate its fate. For the algorithmic trader, this requires constant measurement, active adjustment, and a willingness to let the portfolio's structure—not its recent winners—dictate the balance of risk. The end goal is not just to endure the next downturn, but to remain positioned to exploit whatever opportunities the next market regime brings, without being held hostage by the last one.

### Automating the Safety Net: Explains how to embed risk controls directly into the algorithm

In trading, risk control is not a supplement to strategy—it is the structural foundation that allows a strategy to exist in the first place. A model without an embedded safety net is not a strategy at all; it is an experiment with real capital. Discretionary traders can, at times, rely on instinct to override a bad trade or reduce exposure when markets turn hostile, but algorithms operate without such emotional intuition. They will execute precisely as instructed—no hesitation, no self-doubt, no self-preservation—unless the ability to protect themselves is explicitly coded. *This is both their greatest strength and their most dangerous weakness.* It means that risk controls cannot be an afterthought in the system design process; they must be integrated into the algorithm's logic with the same precision as its entry signals.

Automated safety nets have an advantage over manual intervention: they operate without fatigue, hesitation, or the psychological distortions that plague human decision-making. The key, however, is to ensure that these controls are not simplistic on–off switches, but sophisticated, context-aware mechanisms that can adapt to changing market conditions. A naïve stop-loss function that simply exits at a fixed percentage drawdown may protect against catastrophic collapse, but it will also prematurely cut out of trades during normal volatility spikes, eroding long-term profitability. The real craft lies in building *intelligent* risk modules—ones that can distinguish between routine market noise and genuine structural threats to the portfolio.

One of the most powerful tools for embedding risk discipline directly into algorithms is dynamic position sizing. This mechanism adjusts exposure in real time based on evolving volatility, drawdown levels, or changes in the correlation structure of the portfolio. If volatility in the traded instrument doubles relative to its recent baseline, the algorithm can automatically halve position size, preserving the same risk per trade. If correlations between multiple positions spike during a market stress event, the system can cut aggregate exposure across all affected instruments. This automation prevents the most common trader error: holding full positions in environments where the statistical assumptions underlying the strategy no longer hold.

Another essential safeguard is the inclusion of multi-layered stop and exit protocols. While traditional trading systems might rely on a single stop-loss threshold, more robust algorithmic architectures employ a hierarchy of exits, each triggered by different market or portfolio conditions. The first layer may be a price-based stop tied to technical levels; the second might be a volatility-based exit that triggers if the statistical environment deteriorates; and the third could be a portfolio-wide circuit breaker that liquidates all positions if total drawdown crosses a predetermined percentage. This tiered approach ensures that even if a trade bypasses the first defence, subsequent layers can contain the damage.

Importantly, the automation of these safety nets must account for the fact that markets evolve in ways that static parameters cannot anticipate. A stop-loss level that is optimal in a low-volatility regime may be far too tight during a high-volatility phase, causing a cascade of unnecessary exits. Adaptive algorithms can recalibrate their own parameters based on recent statistical observations, effectively rewriting their own risk profile to remain relevant to the current regime. For example, a volatility stop might be expressed not as a fixed value but as a multiple of the instrument's rolling average true range (ATR), allowing it to flex dynamically as conditions change.

A well-designed automated safety net also extends beyond the trade level to the portfolio as a whole. Many trading systems fail not because individual trades were poorly managed, but because correlated exposures across multiple strategies accumulated silently. By embedding a *portfolio risk monitor* into the algorithmic architecture, the system can continuously assess aggregate exposure, factoring in correlations, leverage, and liquidity constraints. If a portfolio-level metric breaches its risk tolerance—for instance, if expected daily loss exceeds a predefined confidence interval—the algorithm can automatically scale down or halt trading until conditions normalise.

There is also a philosophical element to automation in risk control: deciding what decisions to cede entirely to the machine, and what should remain under human oversight. While full automation is appealing for its consistency, certain rare market events—flash crashes, sudden exchange halts, or geopolitical shocks—can produce market dynamics outside any model's design parameters. Some practitioners favour a *semi-automated* safety net, where the algorithm manages risk within expected regimes, but human intervention is possible for outlier events. Others argue that a fully autonomous system, if well-tested under extreme scenarios, should be trusted over human discretion, given the propensity for fear and greed to erode discipline precisely when it is most needed.

Case studies offer stark lessons. In 2010, during the infamous flash crash, algorithms without embedded portfolio-wide kill switches continued trading into a collapsing market, compounding losses within minutes. In contrast, systems with hard-coded circuit breakers halted all executions once price dislocations exceeded statistical norms. Similarly, during the Swiss National Bank's surprise removal of the euro–franc peg in 2015, some automated FX strategies avoided ruin entirely because their exposure had been dynamically reduced in response to pre-event volatility spikes—a decision made by the algorithm without any explicit awareness of the upcoming policy shock.

Embedding risk controls into algorithms is not simply about preventing blow-ups; it is about shaping the *behavioural profile* of the trading system. A strategy that cuts exposure smoothly as volatility rises will produce a very different equity curve from one that trades full size until a fixed drawdown is hit and then stops abruptly. The former will often see smaller, more manageable losses and be better positioned to resume trading when conditions improve. In this way, risk controls influence not only survival but also recovery speed.

The technical implementation of these safety nets is as important as their conceptual design. Algorithms must monitor risk metrics with minimal latency to avoid executing trades based on stale information. The execution engine must be capable of cancelling or reversing orders immediately when a trigger is hit, even under stressed market conditions where liquidity may be thin. For this reason, many firms separate their risk-control logic from their primary strategy logic, ensuring that a failure in one module does not disable the other. Redundancy and fail-safes are not optional—they are part of the same discipline that underpins the very notion of a safety net.

Ultimately, automating risk control is an act of humility. It is the recognition that no trading model, however sophisticated, is immune to error or to the shifting nature of markets. By embedding defences into the very code that drives execution, a trader accepts that mistakes and surprises are inevitable—but catastrophic ones need not be. The point is not to create a perfect system that never loses money; it is to create a resilient system that can survive its own imperfections long enough to capitalise on its strengths. In algorithmic trading, longevity is the ultimate edge, and automation of the safety net is what makes it possible.

# Chapter 8
# Beating Bias Before It Beats You

Every trader starts with numbers, charts, and economic logic, yet time and again, the deciding factor in outcomes proves far less tangible: the architecture of the mind itself. History is strewn with strategies that were technically sound but undone not by arithmetic errors, but by human psychology. For the retail trader, the battlefield is as much internal as external; it is the cognitive machinery interpreting what the market screen displays. Loss aversion, confirmation bias, recency bias, overconfidence, and the gambler's fallacy are not distant abstractions—they are daily, pervasive forces shaping execution, often beneath conscious awareness. They tip the scales against those who trust in rationality simply because their spreadsheets are flawless. The stark reality is that even the most intelligent participant can, under the right pressures, revert to impulsive speculation.

Here, a well-designed algorithm offers a unique advantage: it does not feel. It does not hesitate after losses, inflate position size after a winning streak, or interpret volatility through the lens of adrenaline. While no human creation is entirely immune to bias, automation can function as a buffer, executing predefined logic when human impulses would otherwise take the wheel. Delegating trade entries and exits to an algorithm is not merely outsourcing labour—it is outsourcing self-control. Yet this delegation is only as robust as the integrity of the code. If bias seeps into design, the system will execute it flawlessly, every time, until capital is eroded.

Many traders stumble here. Believing that stepping away from moment-to-moment execution removes bias entirely is naïve. Bias can emerge long before the click of a trade: in the historical data selected for backtesting, the parameters chosen for optimisation, or the definitions of success and failure used to refine a model. Cherry-picking historical periods that flatter a strategy does not constitute a trivial oversight; it hardwires overconfidence into the algorithm's DNA. Repeatedly tweaking parameters to fit past market quirks does more than tailor a system—it teaches it to mistake yesterday's anomalies for tomorrow's certainties. Automation that should guard now becomes a consistent amplifier of flawed assumptions.

The consequences are systemic. Bias in trading is not merely an operational hazard to manage during execution; it can infiltrate conception, testing, deployment, and monitoring. Mitigation, therefore, must be multi-layered. One layer is the algorithm as shield against impulsive manual trades; another is the disciplined process applied to building, testing, and maintaining that algorithm, ensuring that its logic is not quietly warped by the designer's subconscious preferences. Without both, claims of "bias-free" trading are illusory.

Disciplined review mechanisms are not bureaucratic formalities—they are strategic necessities. A quarterly audit of a trading system, encompassing both performance metrics and design logic, is not about parameter tweaking alone; it is about interrogating underlying assumptions in light of evolving market conditions. Did underperformance arise from structural market shifts or from blind spots in the original design? Are changes being made reactively in response to recent losses, or guided by a statistically justified, forward-looking process? Audits confront the uncomfortable possibility that bias has crept back in, masquerading as reasoned adjustment.

Understanding bias in trading is not memorising cognitive distortions; it is recognising their operational footprints in data selection, code logic, trade frequency, and performance interpretation. It is about creating a workflow where checks against bias are embedded in the very structure of system design, execution, and maintenance. The trader mastering this discipline is not seeking superhuman rationality—they are designing a system that does not demand it.

This chapter examines not only the biases that entrap retail traders, but the structural interventions—human and machine—that constrain their influence before they manifest as costly trades. We explore the algorithm as an emotional buffer, the subtle ways bias infiltrates code, and the systematic review processes that keep these influences in check. The goal is not to eradicate bias—an impossible task—but to reduce its impact to the point where it is negligible, predictable, and manageable. In trading, that difference often separates systems that survive and adapt from those that quietly self-destruct.

## The Psychology of the Retail Trader: Outlines the most common cognitive biases that derail decision-making

The retail trader often imagines themselves as an independent operator—rational, adaptive, and free from the institutional pressures that shape professional market participants. This image is appealing, but it obscures a difficult truth: retail traders are more vulnerable than they realise to the quiet sabotage of cognitive bias. Unlike institutional desks, where decisions are subject to collective scrutiny, a retail trader's choices are typically made in isolation, with no second set of eyes to challenge a faulty inference or emotional impulse. The danger is not simply that bias distorts decision-making; it is that its presence is rarely recognised in the moment. By the time a trader notices its effects, the damage is often embedded in the equity curve. Cognitive bias in trading is not a rare intrusion—it is the default operating mode of the human brain when exposed to uncertainty, risk, and reward. The market is an almost perfect laboratory for triggering the biases that psychologists have documented for decades, and the retail trader is both subject and experimenter. The problem begins with *loss aversion*, the deeply ingrained tendency to fear losses more than valuing equivalent gains. This does not merely encourage premature exits from winning trades; it also tempts traders to hold losing positions in the hope they will return to break-even. The prospect of a small realised loss feels more painful than the abstract possibility of a larger one in the future. In practice, loss aversion causes asymmetry in trade outcomes—profits are cut short while losses are allowed to expand—undermining even strategies with a statistically positive expectancy. The counterpart to this is *overconfidence*, a bias that feeds on early wins, selective memory, and the illusion of control. After a string of profitable trades, a retail trader may overestimate the predictive power of their analysis, underplay the role of chance, and take on positions that exceed prudent risk parameters. Overconfidence often masks itself as conviction, but the two are fundamentally different: conviction is grounded in data and tested logic, while overconfidence is an emotional state that selectively edits reality to support itself. If loss aversion and overconfidence often pull in opposite directions, *confirmation bias* ensures they remain aligned in their destructiveness. This bias pushes traders to seek out, interpret, and remember information that supports their existing view while ignoring contradictory evidence. A trader who believes a particular currency pair is poised to rise will subconsciously discount economic data that undermines this belief and overemphasise technical signals that appear to support it. This creates a feedback loop in which bias-driven trades are reinforced by bias-driven analysis. Then there is *recency bias,* which magnifies the significance of recent events at the expense of the broader historical context. If the market has been trending strongly for the past two weeks, recency bias nudges the trader to believe that such a trend is more likely to continue than it truly is. Conversely, a sudden drawdown may provoke the abandonment of a robust system simply because its most recent trades were losses. Recency bias distorts statistical reasoning by over-weighting the most immediately available outcomes. Another subtle but damaging distortion is the *gambler's fallacy,* the mistaken belief that a deviation from the expected distribution must be "corrected" imminently. In trading, this might manifest as increasing position size after a string of losses under the assumption that a win is now "due," or conversely, becoming risk-averse after consecutive gains out of fear that a loss must be imminent. Both responses mistake randomness for pattern, leading to risk decisions that have no grounding in actual probability. Each of these biases, left unchecked, erodes the trader's ability to act in alignment with a tested methodology. They are not simply psychological curiosities—they have direct, measurable effects on trade selection, position sizing, and the overall equity trajectory. What makes them so insidious is their self-justifying nature: when a bias-driven trade succeeds, it is used as proof of the trader's skill; when it fails, the outcome is often blamed on external conditions rather than the flawed reasoning that produced it. Retail traders, unlike their institutional counterparts, rarely have structured mechanisms to identify and challenge these patterns. The problem is compounded by the immersive nature of trading. The act of monitoring markets in real time exposes traders to a continuous flow of data, much of it noisy, irrelevant, or contradictory. This cognitive load increases the brain's reliance on heuristics—mental shortcuts that are efficient under certain conditions but dangerous in probabilistic environments like markets. The more uncertain and time-pressured the decision, the more likely it is to be driven by bias rather than objective analysis. There are traders who believe that awareness alone is sufficient—that simply knowing about these biases is enough to neutralise them. Experience shows otherwise. Bias operates at a preconscious level, influencing perception before information even reaches the stage of deliberate reasoning. Awareness may allow a trader to recognise bias after the fact, but by then the trade has been placed, the stop-loss set too wide, or the exit delayed in the hope of reversal. The more effective approach is to design structural safeguards into the trading process—rules, checklists, automated executions—that limit the degree to which real-time emotion and perception can alter behaviour. This is not an argument for mechanisation over discretion, but for recognising the limits of human self-control under market conditions. The psychology of the retail trader, then, is not a side topic in trading performance; it is the primary arena in which long-term sustainability is determined. A trading system may be mathematically sound, but if the trader's cognitive biases dictate its application, the theoretical edge is quickly consumed. To trade successfully as a retail participant is to accept that the most formidable market opponent is not another trader or an algorithm—it is the subtle machinery of one's own mind. Understanding these biases in detail is not an academic exercise; it is an operational necessity, because every trade is ultimately filtered through the same fallible human cognition, whether that trade is made manually or coded into an algorithm.

## Algorithm as Emotional Buffer: Shows how automated execution can protect against fear, greed, and impatience

The history of trading is, in large part, the history of human emotion colliding with market uncertainty. Every market cycle leaves behind not only charts and price data but also a trail of behavioural evidence—moments where fear made participants sell too early, greed encouraged them to buy too late, and impatience drove them to abandon carefully considered plans in search of more immediate gratification. These three emotional forces are as old as commerce itself, and they remain among the most consistent reasons why individual traders underperform the very strategies they design. The promise of algorithmic execution is often described in terms of speed, efficiency, or the ability to process vast amounts of data. Yet one of its most significant advantages is not computational at all: it is the ability to enforce discipline in the face of emotional interference. To understand how algorithms serve as an emotional buffer, it is necessary first to examine how emotion undermines performance. Fear in trading is rarely the panic of a market crash; more often it is subtle, arriving as hesitation just as an entry signal appears, or as the impulse to take profits too early because the open position feels too exposed. Greed, its counterpart, is not simply the desire for more money—it is the temptation to increase risk beyond tested parameters after a profitable streak, or to enter trades without sufficient analysis because the recent trend looks irresistible. Impatience, meanwhile, often disguises itself as action-oriented discipline, but in practice it manifests as abandoning a system after a brief drawdown or chasing opportunities outside one's strategy simply because the market appears to be "moving" elsewhere. These responses are not random; they are hardwired into human cognition through evolutionary pressures that have little to do with the statistical nature of markets. In this context, the algorithm does not merely automate a process; it changes the decision architecture. Once rules are coded and execution is delegated to a machine, the psychological feedback loop is altered. The trader no longer has to decide, in real time, whether to pull the trigger on an entry or exit—the algorithm does so without hesitation, without interpreting the latest market fluctuation as personally significant, and without re-evaluating the plan mid-trade based on transient emotional states. This does not mean that emotion disappears entirely; it is shifted earlier in the process, into the design and calibration of the system. That shift is critical. When execution decisions are made at the moment of market engagement, emotion is amplified by immediacy: the P&L changes with every tick, and the trader's perception of risk is shaped by minute-to-minute price action. By moving those decisions into the strategy-development phase—when the trader is not under immediate financial pressure—the algorithm creates a temporal buffer between emotion and execution. This buffer is perhaps most valuable during losing streaks. Humans are loss-averse, and even the most experienced traders feel the psychological weight of consecutive losses.

In discretionary trading, this often leads to "revenge trades" intended to recover losses quickly, or conversely, to excessive caution that prevents valid signals from being taken. An algorithm, by contrast, will continue to execute the tested rules without modification, treating the current losing streak as just another point in the distribution of outcomes. If the system is sound, this behaviour prevents the trader from compounding losses through reactive decision-making. Similarly, in profitable periods, greed can tempt traders to deviate from their plan, often by increasing position sizes or loosening entry criteria in the belief that they are "in sync" with the market. Here too, the algorithm's consistency acts as a counterweight, ensuring that each trade is taken on the same risk terms as before, regardless of recent success. This constancy not only preserves the statistical integrity of the strategy but also prevents the emotional high of winning from distorting perception of probability. It is worth noting that algorithms are not immune to human emotion—they inherit it in their design. The parameters chosen, the indicators prioritised, and the market conditions assumed all reflect human judgement, which may itself be shaped by bias. However, by separating the moments of emotional vulnerability (live trading) from the moments of strategic decision-making (system design), the algorithm minimises the number of emotional "entry points" into the trading process. This is not just a matter of execution speed; it is a matter of cognitive hygiene. In practice, algorithms as emotional buffers are most effective when paired with risk management rules that remove discretionary overrides. A trader who can pause or cancel algorithmic trades at will will still face the temptation to intervene when discomfort peaks. The strongest buffer comes when intervention is minimised, either through psychological discipline or technical constraints that make it cumbersome to interfere without deliberate intent. This design philosophy mirrors practices in aviation and medicine, where automation is used not to replace skilled humans but to prevent them from making predictable, emotionally-driven errors under pressure. The irony is that while many traders are drawn to algorithmic execution for its perceived sophistication, its most valuable function may be its simplicity: it does what it is told, no more, no less, and it does so regardless of whether the last trade was a painful loss or a euphoric win. It does not "feel" the market turning against it, nor does it "sense" an opportunity too good to miss. In a domain where the human mind is both strategist and saboteur, that absence of feeling can be a competitive edge. The broader implication is that algorithmic execution should not be viewed merely as a tool for market analysis or trade timing. It is a structural intervention in the psychology of trading—a way of enforcing adherence to a plan in an environment that is otherwise engineered to provoke impulsive deviation. When fear, greed, and impatience are removed from the moment of execution, the trader is freed from the exhausting cycle of second-guessing and emotional correction, and can instead focus their mental energy on improving the underlying strategy. This reframing is essential: the algorithm is not simply a machine for placing trades; it is a safeguard against the most costly variable in the system—the trader's own emotional interference.

## When Bias Creeps into the Code: Examines how human error still enters algorithm design and how to mitigate it

The popular narrative around algorithmic trading often paints it as a purely rational counterweight to human irrationality—a system immune to the psychological pitfalls that plague discretionary decision-making. Yet this view ignores a critical reality: algorithms are not born from an abstract, bias-free vacuum. They are authored, configured, and iterated by human beings, each carrying their own cognitive blind spots, interpretive frameworks, and behavioural tendencies. The code may execute without emotion, but the logic it embodies can be steeped in the very biases it is meant to protect against. This is not a theoretical hazard—it is a practical and persistent challenge that has undone more algorithmic systems than market randomness ever could. Bias in code can take many forms, but one of the most pervasive is confirmation bias during strategy development. The programmer, consciously or not, may select indicators, timeframes, or filters that support a preconceived market view, discarding or underweighting contradictory evidence. This is especially dangerous in the backtesting phase, where the temptation to "massage" parameters until historical performance appears optimal is both strong and deceptively easy to justify. At its core, this is the same cognitive pattern that leads discretionary traders to interpret ambiguous chart patterns as confirming their existing positions—the only difference is that here, the bias is embedded permanently into the decision rules of a machine. Overfitting is perhaps the most recognisable manifestation of such bias. While often described as a statistical issue, it is fundamentally a human one: the developer's unwillingness to accept that a strategy's performance on historical data may not generalise to the future. The parameters that "just happen" to align perfectly with past price movements may, in reality, be a monument to survivorship bias and selective attention. The risk is that the algorithm's impressive backtest is not a reflection of market truth but of the designer's own cognitive fingerprints. Anchoring bias can also infiltrate the code in subtle ways. A developer might set fixed stop-loss levels, volatility thresholds, or profit targets based on historical regimes they have internalised as "normal," even when those regimes are not representative of current or future market dynamics. This anchoring can limit the adaptability of the algorithm, causing it to underperform in shifting conditions—not because the market is inherently unpredictable, but because the system's design was constrained by outdated mental anchors. There is also a more insidious variant of bias that emerges from the illusion of objectivity. When a decision is encoded in software, it acquires a veneer of neutrality, as if the act of programming it has stripped it of human subjectivity. This can lull developers and stakeholders into overconfidence, underestimating the extent to which the system's behaviour reflects human assumptions, data choices, and interpretations. In practice, this illusion can delay recognition of failure; when trades go wrong, the instinct is to search for external explanations—market anomalies, rare events—rather than questioning whether the bias baked into the logic is the true culprit. Mitigating bias in algorithm design demands more than technical skill; it requires a deliberate, structured approach to challenge the assumptions embedded in every line of code. One effective practice is adversarial testing—developing scenarios or counterfactual datasets specifically designed to disprove the strategy's core thesis. This forces the developer to confront potential weaknesses rather than subconsciously avoiding them. Another safeguard is collaborative or "pair" development, where another quantitative professional reviews the logic not only for errors but for conceptual blind spots. Just as peer review in academic research serves to check the author's interpretations, such collaboration in algorithm design can expose hidden assumptions before they harden into code. The use of walk-forward analysis and out-of-sample testing is often cited as a purely statistical best practice, but its deeper value lies in its ability to break the psychological attachment to historical performance. By repeatedly forcing the strategy to prove itself on unseen data, the developer is reminded that market conditions evolve and that any success tied too tightly to the past is fragile by design. Diversity in data sources is another practical countermeasure. A system trained or calibrated solely on a narrow set of market conditions or instruments is more likely to reflect the biases inherent in those datasets. By incorporating varied markets, timeframes, and volatility regimes into development, the algorithm is exposed to a broader behavioural spectrum, reducing the likelihood that it will be over-tuned to a biased slice of reality. Philosophically, mitigating bias requires accepting that *no algorithm is entirely free of its creator's influence*. The goal is not to achieve some mythical state of perfect objectivity but to recognise, document, and stress-test the assumptions underpinning the strategy. This transparency, whether in personal records or team documentation, becomes essential when revisiting the system months or years later, allowing the developer to recall not just *what* choices were made but *why* they seemed justified at the time. The irony is that many traders turn to automation to escape the unpredictability of human behaviour, yet without vigilance, they end up encoding that very behaviour into their systems—only now it operates at machine speed and scale. The danger of bias in code is not that it exists, but that it is often invisible to the person who wrote it. Overcoming this invisibility requires cultivating a posture of active scepticism toward one's own work, treating every elegant piece of logic as a candidate for disproof until it has been challenged from multiple angles. In the end, algorithms do not fail because they "have emotions" but because they inherit the structural echoes of human fallibility. The most robust systems are not those that assume bias can be eliminated, but those that are built with the expectation that bias will attempt to enter—and with the defences ready to catch it when it does.

### Regular Strategy Audits: Proposes a quarterly review process to catch hidden biases and market shifts

The most sophisticated trading algorithms, no matter how well-engineered at inception, are not immune to degradation over time. Markets are adaptive, complex systems; their participants learn, their structures evolve, and their micro-behaviours shift in response to regulation, technology, and capital flows. What performed flawlessly in one quarter can quietly drift into mediocrity—or outright failure—in the next. Yet such deterioration rarely announces itself in obvious terms. Instead, it creeps in through subtle underperformance, altered volatility patterns, or shifts in liquidity, leaving the unmonitored system vulnerable to mounting losses. This is why a disciplined, recurring process of strategy auditing is not optional; it is the operational equivalent of preventive medicine, catching issues before they metastasise into existential threats.

Quarterly audits offer a pragmatic cadence—frequent enough to identify changes early, yet spaced to avoid reactionary tinkering that would destabilise the strategy. The aim is not to constantly "improve" the algorithm in pursuit of marginal gains, but to confirm that its logic still aligns with market reality and that no unseen bias has crept into its structure or execution. These reviews act as both a health check on the algorithm and a mirror for the developer's own assumptions. Over time, even the most disciplined quant can drift towards justifying a strategy's behaviour based on loyalty to its design rather than objective evidence. The audit's role is to strip away that comfort and subject the system to impartial, structured scrutiny.

A robust review begins with performance dissection beyond headline returns. It asks not only whether the system made or lost money, but whether the distribution of returns, the drawdown patterns, and the win/loss profiles are consistent with its original statistical signature. An algorithm that achieves similar net gains through entirely different trade sequencing may have shifted risk characteristics in ways that the trader would not accept if they were more visible. For instance, a strategy that originally relied on frequent small wins and occasional small losses might, without obvious warning, evolve into one delivering rare large wins and frequent small losses—an entirely different risk profile, masked by a superficially acceptable P&L.

Beyond raw performance, audits must interrogate whether market conditions have materially altered the assumptions on which the system was built. This could mean changes in intraday volatility structure, the dominance of certain participants in the order book, or shifts in cross-asset correlations that invalidate diversification logic. The danger is assuming that because the algorithm's inputs are quantitative, they are immune to qualitative shifts in market behaviour. In reality, such structural changes are often slow-burning and cumulative, visible only when historical data is segmented and examined in rolling windows—a task perfectly suited to the quarterly audit process.

Hidden biases can enter the system post-deployment, not only through coding changes but also through data drift. Data vendors adjust methodologies, tick data feeds degrade in quality during peak loads, and seemingly minor inconsistencies accumulate over months. Left unchecked, these changes can produce a creeping misalignment between the market reality the algorithm believes it is trading and the one in which it is actually operating. A disciplined audit therefore incorporates forensic data validation, ensuring the inputs remain faithful to their original specifications and free from systematic distortion.

The review process is equally concerned with execution quality. A system designed for low-latency execution in deep liquidity conditions may experience rising slippage if liquidity thins or if competition for fills intensifies. Over the span of a few months, this can erode profitability to the point where the underlying strategy logic is sound but the economics no longer justify deployment. The audit identifies these frictional changes, separating signal degradation from cost creep, and informs whether mitigation lies in logic adaptation, execution venue changes, or a shift in order placement tactics.

The quarterly cadence also functions as a safeguard against developer complacency. Once a system is producing steady returns, the temptation is to treat it as a fixed asset rather than a living design. Audits institutionalise scepticism, forcing the developer to treat every positive outcome as something to verify rather than simply to enjoy. This mindset is critical because success, not just failure, can be a fertile ground for bias. Strategies that perform exceptionally well over a short period are particularly vulnerable to survivorship bias—the illusion that strong performance validates the model's robustness when it may simply reflect a temporary alignment between the market's microstructure and the algorithm's idiosyncrasies.

Effective audits are not conducted in isolation by the original developer alone. Independent review—whether by another quant in the same firm or by a trusted external peer—adds a layer of cognitive diversity. It brings in fresh eyes that are less invested in the system's design choices, making it harder for confirmation bias to slip through unchallenged. This mirrors the scientific principle that experimental reproducibility is not guaranteed until another researcher can follow the same methods and arrive at the same results.

It is equally important that the audit process be documented in a way that makes its findings transparent over time. This allows for longitudinal tracking of performance shifts, the persistence of certain anomalies, and the recurrence of specific issues. Without such records, each review risks being a disconnected snapshot, depriving the developer of the ability to detect slow-moving but dangerous trends that emerge only in hindsight.

A quarterly audit is not about undermining confidence in one's systems—it is about building a culture where confidence is earned repeatedly, through evidence. In doing so, it ensures that algorithms are not only responsive to the market they were designed for, but resilient to the market that actually exists today. The trader who neglects this process risks discovering too late that their system's decline was visible long before the damage became irreversible. The trader who embraces it understands that in algorithmic trading, longevity is not about building a perfect strategy once, but about committing to the unglamorous, methodical discipline of keeping it honest.

# Chapter 9
# Scaling Your System Without Losing Control

Growth in algorithmic trading carries a beguiling simplicity on the surface. A system that produces consistent returns naturally tempts its operator to amplify results—larger positions, additional strategies, new markets. Yet scaling is rarely a matter of simple multiplication; it transforms the very fabric of the operation. A strategy that performs flawlessly at modest capacity can become unstable, opaque, or even self-defeating when stretched beyond its limits. The move from "working well" to "working bigger" is not a linear progression—it is a change of state that demands an entirely new set of disciplines.

The first hurdle is recognising when a system is genuinely ready for expansion. Traders often confuse a lucky streak with structural robustness, or a few months of smooth equity curves with statistical reliability. True readiness is demonstrated by stability across varied market conditions, low sensitivity to parameter tweaks, and evidence that the edge is not merely a fleeting quirk of market behaviour. In practice, this entails looking past headline returns to examine the distribution of outcomes, maximum drawdowns under simulated stress, and the system's capacity to maintain performance as volume rises. Premature scaling transforms a healthy strategy into a magnifier of mistakes.

Introducing new strategies into a portfolio is frequently framed as diversification, yet diversification without architectural discipline can create complexity rather than resilience. Fresh algorithms must deliver uncorrelated returns while integrating without destabilising capital allocation, execution pipelines, or monitoring capacity. The hidden pitfalls for ambitious quants often lie not in the quality of individual strategies, but in their interactions: correlations that spike during stress, overlapping orders that strain liquidity, or risk controls never designed for multi-strategy contexts. Safe scaling is therefore less about adding everything possible and more about layering deliberately, with visibility into each element's interaction with the whole.

As systems expand, so too does complexity, often eroding the trader's understanding of their own infrastructure. A single, elegant model is manageable; a network of interconnected strategies, execution scripts, and failover systems can quickly become opaque. This opacity carries subtle danger: unexpected behaviour becomes harder to diagnose, and the operator's sense of control begins to slip. Complexity cannot be eliminated entirely—growth invariably introduces more moving parts—but it can be constrained to a level that remains comprehensible. Clear documentation, modular design, and consistent architectural principles become as essential as the alpha-generating logic itself.

The lure of over-automation adds another layer of risk. With sufficient programming skill, systems can monitor themselves, adapt parameters in real time, and execute autonomously. On paper, this promises efficiency; in practice, it can produce a black box even its creator cannot fully explain. The danger is both philosophical and practical: if you cannot articulate why the system makes its decisions, you have surrendered the role of trader to a process you cannot interrogate. The boundary between effective automation and abdication of responsibility is narrow, often crossed unnoticed—until a costly failure occurs.

Successful scaling demands restraint, particularly in the pursuit of speed and capacity. Growth must be matched by oversight, diagnostic capability, and the trader's comprehension of the ecosystem they are expanding. Scaling is about constructing a framework capable of carrying more weight without buckling, rather than piling onto a fragile foundation. The crucial question is not merely "how big can I make this?" but "how far can I expand while still being able to explain, control, and refine every component?" Mastery lies in scaling without surrendering understanding or authority.

### Knowing When You're Ready: Explains the performance and stability signals that justify scaling up

The most dangerous moment for a trading system is not its first live trade, nor its first losing streak—it is the point at which it begins to work well enough to tempt expansion. At that juncture, the human mind is particularly vulnerable to a subtle bias: the conflation of recent success with enduring capability. Traders eager to "take the brakes off" often misread short-term performance as proof of structural soundness, leading them to scale a system that has not yet been battle-tested. Knowing when you are truly ready to scale is less about excitement and more about disciplined recognition of signals that confirm a system's resilience, adaptability, and operational integrity.

The first of these signals is performance robustness across diverse market conditions. A profitable system in one market regime tells you almost nothing about how it will behave when volatility spikes, liquidity dries up, or correlations shift suddenly. Scaling before the system has survived a representative set of conditions is akin to assuming a prototype bridge will handle heavy freight simply because it carried a single car. Stress testing must move beyond historical backtests into simulated extreme scenarios—sharp drawdowns, correlated market crashes, flash liquidity gaps—designed to expose fragilities before they are amplified. A system that can weather these tests without collapsing in execution efficiency or risk profile demonstrates a form of readiness that raw returns alone cannot prove.

Equally important is statistical stability. Too often, traders assess readiness by looking only at headline performance metrics such as total return or Sharpe ratio, ignoring whether those numbers are being driven by a handful of outsized trades. A system that relies on a small cluster of rare events is inherently fragile; scale it, and the law of large numbers works against you. Instead, readiness should be signalled by a healthy distribution of returns, low variance in win rates across different market environments, and resilience to modest parameter changes. The latter is crucial: if a small tweak in lookback period or execution timing turns a strong performer into a consistent loser, the edge is more brittle than it appears. Robust systems exhibit what could be called *topographical stability*—small variations in design do not produce cliffs in performance.

Operational reliability is another underappreciated component of scaling readiness. It is one thing for a trading model to generate profitable signals; it is quite another for the surrounding infrastructure—data feeds, execution gateways, monitoring systems—to process greater volume without delays, errors, or missed fills. Scaling up magnifies not only financial exposure but also the frequency and severity of operational glitches. Traders who assess readiness solely through the lens of backtested equity curves risk overlooking whether their systems can handle an order flow ten times larger, or whether latency-sensitive strategies will degrade when execution venues are saturated. A realistic readiness assessment includes dry-run simulations of scaled execution to reveal bottlenecks before they cost real capital.

Capital sufficiency must also be considered in light of risk tolerance, not just opportunity. Scaling a strategy without proportional capital to buffer expected drawdowns leads to psychological stress and premature abandonment of otherwise viable systems. The key is not merely having "more money to deploy," but having enough capital to maintain conviction through the scaled system's statistically probable worst-case drawdown. If a trader finds themselves at the edge of their emotional tolerance with current position sizes, they are not ready to scale—because scaling will magnify not just profits and losses, but also the psychological strain of drawdown periods.

Another critical readiness marker is monitoring capability. A scaled system demands sharper, more proactive oversight, particularly if multiple strategies or markets are involved. Traders often underestimate the cognitive load of supervising larger, more complex operations. The ability to detect anomalies quickly—be it an execution lag, an unexplained strategy deviation, or a divergence from expected correlation behaviour—is what prevents small errors from cascading into large losses. The readiness question here is: do you have the tools, dashboards, and alert mechanisms to maintain real-time situational awareness at scale? If not, readiness remains theoretical.

One of the most overlooked signs of readiness is the trader's own detachment from outcome bias. Scaling should be driven by evidence of structural resilience, not by the emotional high of a recent winning streak. If a decision to scale feels urgent, it is likely premature. The discipline to wait until multiple independent indicators—performance stability, operational capacity, risk-buffer adequacy, monitoring readiness—align is itself a readiness signal. This restraint indicates the trader is operating from a strategic mindset rather than reactive impulse, a necessary trait for sustaining performance under greater exposure.

There is also the matter of *external alignment*. Scaling is not performed in a vacuum; market conditions, broker stability, counterparty reliability, and regulatory environments all influence whether now is the right moment. A system might be internally ready but face external risks that make scaling ill-timed—such as upcoming market structure changes, rising transaction costs, or liquidity contractions in the targeted asset class. The readiness question extends beyond "can my system handle it?" to "will the market environment allow my system to handle it effectively right now?"

The philosophical challenge is that readiness is rarely a single, unambiguous moment. It is an accumulation of evidence from multiple dimensions: robustness, stability, capacity, discipline, and environmental fit. Traders who treat readiness as a box-ticking exercise risk ignoring the nuanced interactions between these factors. A system might be technically ready but not operationally supported, or operationally sound but psychologically fragile in its management. Only when these dimensions converge—without reliance on any one to carry the others—can scaling be justified without courting disaster.

Ultimately, knowing when you're ready is not about eliminating all risk; scaling always introduces new vulnerabilities. Rather, it is about ensuring that the vulnerabilities you face are intentional, measured, and within your capacity to absorb—financially, operationally, and mentally. The temptation to scale will appear long before the evidence of readiness is complete. The edge belongs to those who can resist that temptation until the signals are not just promising, but compelling.

## Adding Strategies Safely: Shows how to layer new algorithms without destabilising your portfolio

The temptation to add a new algorithm often emerges from the same place as the desire to scale: the sense that what you have is working, and more of it—different, smarter, faster—must be better. But in portfolio construction, the mathematics of diversification is less forgiving than its theory suggests. A single poorly integrated strategy can undermine years of disciplined gains, not because it is inherently unprofitable, but because it interacts with the existing ecosystem in ways you did not anticipate. Safety in this context is not a conservative refusal to innovate, but a disciplined process for ensuring that new strategies expand your opportunity set without eroding the structural integrity of your portfolio.

The first principle is that new strategies must be evaluated not in isolation but in their *full interaction* with what you already run. It is easy to be seduced by an algorithm's standalone backtest, showing smooth equity curves and enviable Sharpe ratios. Yet those curves tell you little about how the strategy will behave when layered into an environment with shared liquidity pools, overlapping exposure patterns, and correlated execution timing. A system that performs well on its own but doubles your exposure to specific risk factors—be it volatility spikes in emerging markets or mean-reversion bets in high-beta equities—can destabilise the entire portfolio. This is why forward-looking correlation analysis is not optional.

Historical correlation may offer a baseline, but robustness requires scenario-based stress testing that imagines what happens when correlations break down in crisis conditions.

Secondly, the sequencing of introduction matters. New strategies should be deployed in controlled increments, with deliberately reduced capital allocation during their observation phase. This is not only to limit downside risk, but to capture operational learning: how does the strategy's real-time behaviour align with its simulated profile? Are its slippage and latency sensitivities consistent with expectations? Does it create queue priority conflicts with other algorithms, or distort market impact profiles when traded in conjunction with them? Such questions cannot be fully answered in backtests because the live trading environment is dynamic and adaptive—your own activity can alter the market's microstructure in ways that feed back into execution outcomes.

A third, often underappreciated, dimension is operational compatibility. Each algorithm brings its own demands—data refresh intervals, computational intensity, position monitoring needs—and these can strain shared infrastructure. Introducing a strategy that requires high-frequency recalculations into a platform optimised for mid-frequency trend-following can lead to bottlenecks or increased latency for all strategies, not just the new one. This is particularly true when scaling across multiple asset classes where market data formats, tick sizes, and trading hours differ substantially. Operational readiness checks must go beyond whether the algorithm's logic is sound; they must assess whether the ecosystem can support it without degradation.

Risk concentration is rarely obvious at first glance. Traders often focus on asset-level diversification—adding a fixed-income mean-reversion strategy to an equity trend-following portfolio, for example—without recognising that both may be indirectly sensitive to the same macroeconomic drivers, such as central bank policy or energy price shocks. A rigorous risk factor decomposition is essential, identifying not just direct exposures but also the second-order relationships that emerge under stress. The aim is not to eliminate shared risk entirely—that is impossible—but to ensure that the contribution of any single factor to total portfolio variance remains contained, even under adverse conditions.

Another subtle danger lies in behavioural coupling between strategies. Algorithms that share decision-making frameworks, even when trading different markets, can enter or exit positions at similar times if they are reacting to common volatility or momentum triggers. This synchronisation effect, especially under market stress, can magnify drawdowns and erode liquidity when you most need it. The solution is deliberate desynchronisation—varying signal lookbacks, execution schedules, or capital activation thresholds to reduce unintended clustering of trades. This requires not just statistical analysis but a design philosophy that prioritises independence of signal generation wherever possible.

The process of safe integration also demands an honest assessment of your monitoring and intervention capacity. Every additional strategy increases the cognitive and operational load on the trader or risk manager. A portfolio with three algorithms can be monitored intuitively; a portfolio with fifteen cannot. The sophistication of your oversight tools—alert systems, anomaly detection algorithms, real-time P&L attribution—must evolve proportionally with the number of strategies. Without this scaling of oversight, the incremental risk from complexity can outweigh the incremental benefit from diversification.

Furthermore, the decision to add a strategy should be governed by a clear set of inclusion criteria that extend beyond projected returns. These criteria might include complementary risk factor exposure, acceptable drawdown correlation with existing strategies, manageable incremental infrastructure demands, and demonstrable live-test stability over a minimum period. Formalising such criteria protects against the allure of "shiny object" strategies—those that look appealing in the short term but do not materially improve the long-term robustness of the portfolio.

Crucially, safe addition is as much about readiness to *remove* as it is about readiness to add. A new strategy should not be viewed as a permanent fixture but as a candidate on probation, subject to defined performance and risk review intervals. The decision to deactivate must be as unemotional and process-driven as the decision to onboard, preventing sunk-cost bias from keeping underperforming or destabilising algorithms in production long after their edge has eroded.

Layering algorithms is ultimately an exercise in architecture, not accumulation. The portfolio is a living system, and every new element changes the way it breathes, responds, and sustains itself under stress. Safety does not mean avoiding new strategies; it means ensuring that each addition strengthens the system's adaptability rather than stretching it to fragility. The discipline lies in recognising that the success of a multi-strategy approach is determined less by the brilliance of any single algorithm and more by the coherence of the whole—and coherence is something that must be designed, not assumed.

## Managing Complexity: Teaches the art of keeping systems understandable as they grow

Complexity in algorithmic trading systems does not arrive all at once; it creeps in incrementally, camouflaged as progress. A small modification to signal logic here, an additional risk overlay there, a new data feed integrated to capture a perceived edge—each step seems reasonable and even prudent. Yet over time, the cumulative effect can transform a system that was once transparent and elegant into an opaque machine whose behaviour you can no longer fully explain. This is not merely an aesthetic problem. In trading, *what you cannot explain, you cannot control,* and the loss of explainability is one of the most dangerous forms of risk you can introduce into your portfolio.

A system's growth should therefore be guided not just by the pursuit of performance gains but by the preservation of structural clarity. This begins with understanding that complexity has both visible and invisible dimensions. The visible complexity lies in the codebase: lines of logic, the number of modules, the interdependencies between functions. The invisible complexity resides in the mental model required to operate and oversee the system effectively. A trader can tolerate a large and intricate codebase if the conceptual map—the "why" and "how" of each component—remains intact in their mind. It is when the code and the conceptual map drift apart that the risk of systemic failure multiplies.

One of the most effective ways to manage this drift is to enforce a discipline of *design transparency*. Every new feature, however small, should come with a clear, documented rationale, the specific conditions under which it is expected to add value, and the criteria for its removal should those conditions change. This is more than bureaucracy—it creates an audit trail of intent, enabling you to revisit decisions months or years later with the original context intact. Without such documentation, traders often find themselves defending features that no longer serve their intended purpose, kept alive simply because no one remembers why they were introduced or what might break if they are removed.

Complexity also demands that you recognise the limits of your own cognitive bandwidth. As the number of strategies, markets, and data sources grows, the human brain's capacity to hold all relevant interactions in working memory diminishes. This is where monitoring and diagnostic tools must evolve in parallel with system growth. Real-time dashboards, anomaly detection algorithms, and performance attribution frameworks are not luxuries; they are cognitive prosthetics, enabling you to maintain a coherent mental model without being overwhelmed by raw data. The best of these tools do not just report numbers; they surface the relationships and dependencies that matter most, allowing you to see emerging problems before they metastasise into losses.

However, tools alone cannot compensate for poor architectural choices. A scalable, understandable system is one in which components are modular and loosely coupled, so that changes in one part have minimal unintended consequences elsewhere. Overly intertwined systems are like tightly wound knots—pull on one strand and the entire structure shifts in unpredictable ways. Modularity not only makes debugging and upgrades simpler; it also allows for partial system failures without collapsing the whole. In trading terms, this means a faulty execution module can be taken offline without halting risk management functions, or a single underperforming strategy can be paused without disrupting unrelated positions.

Another key discipline is *simplicity bias*—a conscious preference for the simplest effective solution to any problem. Complexity tends to accumulate when traders and developers overfit to recent data or add redundant layers of filtering in pursuit of marginal gains. The irony is that these additions often increase fragility, making the system more sensitive to data quality issues, latency fluctuations, or market regime shifts. A simplicity bias forces you to justify every additional rule, signal, or dataset not just by its backtested returns but by the incremental resilience it brings to the overall architecture. If the benefit is purely cosmetic or narrowly conditional, it is likely not worth the cognitive and operational cost.

Scaling a trading system also means scaling the processes that keep it intelligible. Code reviews, cross-training among team members, and scheduled "debrief" sessions where each strategy is explained from first principles are not just procedural hygiene—they are safeguards against institutional memory loss. In fast-moving firms, staff turnover or even role changes can sever the chain of understanding that connects a system's current state to its original design philosophy. Without deliberate mechanisms to transfer knowledge, complexity can outlive the people who created it, leaving successors to manage a black box whose failure modes are unknown.

Yet the pursuit of understandability must be balanced against the reality that some complexity is not only unavoidable but necessary. Multi-strategy, multi-asset portfolios inherently involve interacting timeframes, heterogeneous data structures, and adaptive parameters. The art lies in distinguishing between *essential* complexity—the irreducible detail required to capture and manage diverse opportunities—and *accidental* complexity, which arises from poor integration, redundant processes, or untested assumptions. The former is an investment in capability; the latter is a liability in disguise.

Managing complexity also requires the humility to acknowledge that control is not binary but probabilistic. Even the best-designed systems will occasionally behave in unexpected ways, especially when market conditions deviate sharply from historical norms. The goal is not to eliminate surprises entirely—that is impossible—but to ensure that when surprises occur, they can be diagnosed quickly and corrected with minimal disruption. This is why *explainability* should be treated as a functional requirement, not an afterthought. If you cannot explain in plain language why a system just entered or exited a trade, you are no longer the system's master; you are its hostage.

Ultimately, the art of managing complexity is the art of preserving agency. It is about ensuring that as your systems grow in scope and sophistication, they remain tools that serve your strategic vision rather than autonomous constructs you are forced to follow blindly. This requires constant vigilance, disciplined design, and a willingness to prune as aggressively as you build. For in trading, as in all complex domains, *it is not the biggest system that wins, but the one whose operators understand it well enough to keep it from defeating itself.*

## The Dangers of Over-Automation: Warns against ceding too much control to systems you can't explain

There is a seduction in automation that is as powerful as it is dangerous. It offers the trader a vision of flawless execution, tireless monitoring, and instantaneous reaction to market changes—a machine that works while you sleep, immune to fatigue, distraction, or emotion. Yet history in both finance and technology is littered with examples where over-reliance on systems that could not be fully explained led to catastrophic outcomes. The problem is not automation itself, but the surrender of agency that often follows: the gradual shift from using the machine as a tool to obeying it as an oracle. *When you no longer understand the reasoning behind a system's actions, you have ceded the ability to intervene meaningfully when things go wrong.*

The allure of "hands-off" trading is easy to understand. Complex algorithms can process volumes of data no human could analyse in real time, spot fleeting opportunities invisible to the naked eye, and react in milliseconds. For certain market environments, such advantages can be decisive. But automation also creates a psychological trap. As the system demonstrates competence and reliability over time, oversight can become perfunctory. Wins are credited to its sophistication, while losses are rationalised as anomalies. Slowly, the human operator shifts from active steward to passive monitor, watching without truly understanding. This erosion of understanding is the first step toward vulnerability.

Consider the flash crash of 6 May 2010, when US equity markets plunged and rebounded within minutes, wiping hundreds of billions in market value before anyone had time to process what was happening. While multiple factors were involved, the event illustrated how automated trading systems, interacting in ways their designers did not anticipate, could create feedback loops beyond human comprehension in real time. More importantly, it showed that even highly regulated markets with sophisticated participants were not immune to sudden destabilisation driven by algorithms acting faster than human oversight could respond. In such moments, the inability to explain why the system is behaving as it is turns the trader into a spectator of their own portfolio's fate.

The risk is compounded when the underlying logic of an automated system is opaque not just in speed but in structure. Many machine learning-based strategies, for instance, rely on models whose decision pathways are not easily interpretable. While these models can be extraordinarily effective in pattern recognition, their very strength—finding non-linear relationships in vast datasets—makes them resistant to post-hoc explanation. Without explainability, you cannot determine whether a sudden drop in performance is due to market regime change, a data feed anomaly, or the model itself overfitting to noise. This lack of diagnostic clarity can lead to either paralysis—doing nothing while losses mount—or reckless intervention that disrupts legitimate trades.

Over-automation also creates hidden dependencies that magnify operational risk. A system might appear autonomous, but it relies on external data sources, infrastructure stability, and integration with brokers or exchanges. When these dependencies fail, the fallout can be far greater if human operators have not maintained the ability to step in and operate—or wind down—the system manually. In 2012, Knight Capital Group famously lost $440 million in 45 minutes due to a software deployment error that interacted with dormant code. The systems executed trades exactly as they were programmed, but no one could intervene fast enough because the human operators had been effectively sidelined by years of trusting automated execution.

There is also a subtler danger: the atrophy of human skill. A trader who leans too heavily on automated systems risks losing the ability to think critically about markets in real time. The more you outsource decision-making to machines, the less you practise the pattern recognition, scenario analysis, and adaptive thinking that define professional judgement. This erosion is gradual, and often invisible until the moment the system falters and you are forced to act independently. By then, your reflexes and analytical instincts may be too rusty to match the speed and clarity the situation demands.

Guarding against over-automation does not mean reverting to manual trading. It means designing systems with *explainability, intervention points, and human-in-the-loop capabilities as core principles rather than afterthoughts*. Explainability ensures that the system's actions can be traced to intelligible inputs and rules. Intervention points allow human operators to pause, adjust, or override automated decisions without dismantling the entire architecture. Human-in-the-loop design treats automation as augmentation, not replacement—leveraging machines for what they do best while retaining human discretion for high-impact, ambiguous situations.

One practical safeguard is the use of *shadow modes* when deploying new strategies or updates. In this configuration, the system runs in parallel with live markets but does not execute real trades, allowing the operator to observe and understand its behaviour under current conditions. Such an approach not only catches technical errors before they cost money but also deepens the operator's familiarity with the system's decision-making logic. Over time, this familiarity becomes a buffer against blind trust.

Another safeguard is the regular practice of scenario drills—structured exercises in which human operators simulate sudden market shocks, data outages, or system malfunctions and rehearse intervention protocols. These drills serve two purposes: they keep manual skills sharp, and they expose weaknesses in both system design and human readiness before those weaknesses are tested under real pressure. The most robust trading operations treat these drills not as optional insurance but as a core component of risk management.

Philosophically, the central discipline is resisting the narrative that "the system knows best." Algorithms are powerful precisely because they are single-minded in execution, but markets are complex, adaptive systems in which rules that worked yesterday can fail spectacularly tomorrow. A system's historical performance is not evidence of its infallibility; it is merely a record of how it behaved under a particular set of conditions. The moment those conditions change, your ability to explain and adapt becomes the difference between resilience and ruin.

In the end, automation should be a partner, not a master. The goal is not to build a system that runs without you but to build one that runs with you—leveraging computational precision while preserving human oversight, curiosity, and accountability. The danger is not in the code itself but in the abdication of responsibility that can accompany it. A trader who understands every critical component of their system can use automation to extend their reach and sharpen their edge. One who cannot explain it is not truly trading at all—they are gambling on the hope that the machine will remain benevolent. History suggests that is a hope best tempered with vigilance.

# Chapter 10
# The Edge in a Changing Market

The advantage you possess today is rarely the one you can rely on tomorrow. Markets are not static; they evolve in ways both overt and subtle, shaped by shifts in liquidity, regulation, technology, and human behaviour. Signals that once seemed dependable can erode slowly over months or vanish entirely in the span of a single news cycle. Algorithmic trading systems, despite their speed and precision, are just as exposed to these dynamics as discretionary traders. The crucial difference is that while a human might detect change through intuition or observation, a machine will continue executing its programmed rules until explicitly adjusted. In a shifting market, the true edge lies not in constructing a flawless system, but in cultivating the agility to adapt that system before obsolescence forces your hand.

Adaptation begins with recognising that market regimes—periods dominated by specific relationships, volatilities, and behaviours—are inherently temporary. A contraction in volatility that favours mean-reversion strategies can abruptly give way to a breakout environment, leaving the same strategies bleeding capital. Liquidity profiles shift as participants enter or exit, altering execution dynamics in ways that historical models may never anticipate. Even correlations between asset classes, such as equities and bonds, can reverse under different macroeconomic conditions. For the algorithmic trader, detecting these regime changes early and recalibrating models accordingly often distinguishes compounding gains from a slow, invisible slide into irrelevance.

Yet adaptation is not a purely technical exercise. Market data are the outputs of a world animated by human narratives—economic cycles, political shifts, and cultural events that frame behaviour. An algorithm optimised for stability might perform admirably until an election, policy change, or geopolitical shock introduces structural volatility. Recognising when these broader narratives should influence algorithmic parameters is a subtle skill. Overreact, and you risk overfitting to fleeting noise; underreact, and you miss the inflection points that redefine the playing field. The challenge is weaving narrative awareness into a quantitative framework without sacrificing discipline or succumbing to subjective bias.

Continuous learning is the anchor that tempers both complacency and overreaction. Markets constantly present more data, novel tools, and emerging methodologies than any single team can fully master. Selective curiosity becomes essential. Staying current does not mean chasing every new API, machine learning technique, or exotic dataset. It entails periodically reviewing your toolkit, assessing your skills, and auditing your systems to ensure they remain fit for purpose—retiring or upgrading components that no longer meet the standard. In this context, the sophistication of your system matters far less than the discernment applied to what belongs in it.

The temptation to over-adapt—to pursue every trend under the guise of staying ahead—is as perilous as clinging rigidly to outdated methods. New tools can offer genuine opportunity, but they can just as easily introduce complexity, cost, and fragility without adding real edge. Many traders have undermined profitable systems by layering untested signals or integrating novel data sources merely because they were fashionable. Others have devoted months to embedding a cutting-edge library, only to find it offers no meaningful improvement over methods already well understood. Discipline lies in adopting change not for novelty, but in service of a clearly defined strategic objective.

Maintaining an edge in a mutable market requires recognising that both the market and your system are living, evolving entities in constant dialogue. The most effective traders are not those who predict the future with precision, but those who perceive the present clearly and act decisively. They build systems resilient enough to evolve without collapsing under the weight of every adjustment, while cultivating the judgement to distinguish adaptation that strengthens from change that distracts. In the chapters ahead, we will explore how to retrain and recalibrate algorithms for shifting regimes, how to integrate human narrative into quantitative systems without distortion, how to sustain a disciplined learning habit, and how to resist the seductive pull of every new innovation. Because in markets that never cease to change, the real edge is not the trade you place today—it is your ability to remain effective, adaptable, and informed tomorrow.

## Adapting to New Market Regimes: Explains how algorithms can be retrained or adjusted for shifting conditions

Every trading system is built on the implicit assumption that the relationships it exploits will hold for a useful period of time. This is the foundation on which models are trained, tested, and deployed. Yet the reality is that financial markets do not simply fluctuate in random noise around a stable mean; they shift in fundamental ways that can render yesterday's logic obsolete. Recognising and adapting to these market regime changes is not an optional skill—it is the core discipline that separates systems that survive from those that decay. An algorithm might have a Sharpe ratio of 2.0 in backtests spanning a decade, but if that decade sits inside a single dominant regime, the real challenge begins the moment the underlying structure changes.

Market regimes are defined by persistent patterns in volatility, correlation, liquidity, and macroeconomic drivers. They might be long—such as the low-interest-rate expansion of the 2010s—or painfully short, like the compressed volatility in certain equity markets during brief pre-crisis lulls. The shift between regimes often comes with warning signs: volatility clustering, breakdowns in previously stable correlations, widening spreads in fixed income, or unusual behaviour in safe-haven assets. The trouble for algorithmic traders is that these signals rarely arrive neatly labelled. They emerge as statistical anomalies that can be dismissed as noise until the change becomes undeniable. *The cost of waiting for confirmation is that by the time you have certainty, your system's performance may have already deteriorated beyond repair.*

Effective adaptation begins with detection. Some practitioners rely on statistical techniques—such as rolling window performance metrics, volatility regime-switching models, or change-point detection algorithms—to flag structural shifts in market behaviour. Others integrate macroeconomic indicators or even text analysis of news flows to sense changing conditions. Neither is sufficient alone. A purely statistical approach can be late to respond or over-sensitive to false positives; a narrative-driven approach risks introducing subjective bias. The most resilient frameworks combine both: they let the data drive the recognition of potential change, while informed human judgement assesses whether the signal aligns with real-world catalysts.

Once a regime shift is identified, retraining an algorithm is not simply a matter of feeding it new data. The core question is whether the underlying strategy logic is still valid in the new environment. Mean-reversion models may collapse in sustained trending conditions; momentum systems can suffer in choppy, low-volatility markets. Retraining on recent data without evaluating strategic fit risks overfitting to a transient phase. In practice, the best approach is a staged response: first, reduce position sizing or exposure while assessing stability; second, run the existing system in parallel with an updated candidate model; finally, transition only when the new system demonstrates durability across both recent and stress-tested historical scenarios.

Case studies reveal how costly neglect can be. Quant funds that built their models during the extended low-volatility years preceding 2007 suffered heavily when credit conditions tightened and volatility regimes shifted almost overnight. Their algorithms, calibrated for stable spreads and steady liquidity, began executing in a market where execution cost assumptions no longer held. In contrast, the managers who had regime-monitoring triggers—such as adaptive volatility scaling or liquidity-sensitive execution logic—were able to throttle exposure and re-optimise models before the full impact hit. *Adaptation is not only about restoring profitability; it is equally about preserving capital during periods of uncertainty.*

Retraining also requires thinking beyond the model itself. Data inputs that were once predictive may lose signal strength or even become misleading. A factor that worked in one regime might invert in another, turning a strength into a liability. Feature engineering should therefore be part of the adaptation process, with rigorous evaluation of whether each variable retains its predictive relevance. This is where domain knowledge matters: statistical correlation alone is not enough; one must understand the economic or behavioural mechanism that made the factor relevant in the first place, and whether that mechanism still operates.

Technology plays a dual role in this process. On the one hand, advances in machine learning and cloud computing allow for faster retraining and more sophisticated scenario testing. On the other, the ease of recomputation can tempt teams into frequent, reactionary retraining that destabilises a system. *The discipline lies in adapting only when there is evidence of a structural shift, not simply because the last two weeks were unfavourable.* This is a point where experienced practitioners diverge from novices—the latter often confuse short-term drawdowns with regime shifts, while the former look for persistent, cross-metric confirmation before making structural changes.

One often overlooked aspect is that adaptation need not always mean a wholesale redesign. Sometimes the regime change affects only a segment of the trading environment, allowing for modular adjustments: changing execution timing, recalibrating stop-loss thresholds, or altering portfolio weighting schemes can extend a system's viability without dismantling its core. The advantage of modularity is that it allows for partial adaptation while preserving the stability of proven components, reducing the risk of unintentional breakage.

From a philosophical standpoint, adapting to market regimes requires accepting impermanence as the default state of the system–market relationship. It demands humility to admit that no model, no matter how elegantly engineered, is immune to decay. This humility must be balanced with the resolve to act decisively when conditions change. The trader who is slow to adapt risks irrelevance; the one who adapts too readily risks thrashing their own system into mediocrity. The art lies in maintaining that tension—constantly prepared to pivot, yet anchored in evidence and process.

Ultimately, regime adaptation is less about predicting the future than about recognising when the present has changed enough to invalidate the past. The traders who master this do not think in terms of defending a static edge; they think in terms of managing a dynamic one. They build systems with the agility to be retrained, the monitoring to detect when retraining is necessary, and the discipline to make changes only when the evidence is compelling. In a world where market structure can shift faster than a quarterly report, this ability to adapt becomes not just a competitive advantage, but the prerequisite for survival.

## The Role of Human Narrative: Discusses when broader economic, political, or cultural narratives should influence algorithm settings

Markets are not sterile arenas driven solely by data streams and execution logic. They are social systems, fuelled by human behaviour, shaped by collective psychology, and often moved by stories that have little to do with quantifiable fundamentals—at least in the short term. The danger for a purely algorithmic trader is assuming that price action alone contains all relevant information, ignoring the fact that markets can pivot abruptly when a political decision, an economic policy shift, or a cultural event captures global attention. Algorithms excel at exploiting measurable patterns, but they do not, by default, understand why those patterns exist or when a new narrative might erode them. *A well-tuned system can be blindsided not by statistical noise, but by a human story strong enough to redefine the rules.*

The most illustrative examples often occur during political crises. Consider the sterling's behaviour in the weeks before and after the Brexit referendum. Models trained on years of relatively stable GBP volatility were utterly unprepared for the sudden repricing of risk that followed the vote. The shift was not gradual; it was driven by a single, binary event whose probability and consequences were fiercely debated in public discourse. An algorithm ignorant of that narrative would have treated the spike as an outlier or temporary dislocation, potentially taking positions in anticipation of mean reversion that never materialised. Traders who incorporated the political narrative—adjusting exposure, widening risk parameters, or temporarily disabling certain strategies—were better positioned to survive the turbulence.

Economic narratives can be subtler but equally powerful. A shift in central bank policy, for instance, may not immediately change the data in your model, yet it alters market participants' expectations in ways that ripple through pricing. When the U.S. Federal Reserve signalled a transition from quantitative easing to tightening, the bond market began re-pricing well before the data on inflation or growth fully justified the move. Here, the narrative acted as a leading indicator, one that models trained solely on lagging data would have failed to capture in time. Recognising the story behind the numbers is often the difference between positioning ahead of the move and reacting after the fact.

Cultural narratives are harder to measure but cannot be dismissed. In the technology sector, for example, investor enthusiasm can be driven by prevailing societal fascination with a theme—be it artificial intelligence, renewable energy, or blockchain. During the cryptocurrency boom of 2017, and again in 2020–2021, price surges in digital assets were propelled as much by the social narrative of financial revolution as by any measurable improvement in adoption metrics. In such cases, algorithms rooted in valuation or transaction flow data would have struggled to explain the speed and magnitude of price increases. Traders who understood the cultural momentum behind the market could adjust their systems to account for higher volatility regimes or altered correlations.

Integrating narrative into algorithmic trading is not a call to abandon objectivity; it is a call to recognise that *narratives are themselves market variables*, albeit ones that are qualitative, fluid, and often loosely defined. The key is to decide when the narrative's strength and relevance justify altering system parameters. One approach is to set explicit triggers for narrative-aware interventions: for instance, defining that certain categories of events—central bank announcements, election outcomes, major geopolitical conflicts—warrant a formal review of position limits or volatility assumptions. This transforms the integration of human narrative from a discretionary impulse into a structured, repeatable process.

There is also the risk of overfitting to narrative. Markets are full of stories, and most of them do not matter in the way commentators think they do. Headlines can exaggerate, social media can amplify noise, and investor sentiment can swing on inconsequential developments. Traders must guard against the temptation to tweak algorithms in response to every compelling headline. The discipline lies in distinguishing between *narrative as entertainment* and *narrative as a structural force*. The former generates clicks and short-term volatility; the latter reshapes the market's operating conditions for weeks, months, or years.

Quantitative tools can aid this judgement. Natural language processing (NLP) models can measure the frequency, sentiment, and thematic consistency of news and social media coverage, offering an objective proxy for narrative intensity. By correlating this data with past market behaviour during similar narrative cycles, traders can calibrate when intervention is statistically justified. This does not replace human judgement—it sharpens it, allowing the trader to act not on vague impressions but on measurable evidence that the story has reached a level of market-wide significance.

The best practitioners treat human narrative as a strategic overlay, not a constant driver of decision-making. In stable, predictable regimes, letting the algorithm run without narrative interference preserves its statistical edge. But in moments when the collective attention of the market is so focused on a single story that liquidity, volatility, and correlation structures are likely to shift, narrative awareness becomes a form of risk management. This is not just about preventing losses; it is about ensuring the algorithm is not operating on assumptions that the market has already abandoned.

Ultimately, the role of human narrative in algorithmic trading is a test of intellectual flexibility. It challenges the trader to operate in two modes simultaneously: the rigorous, data-driven discipline of quantitative analysis, and the adaptive, context-sensitive awareness of a macro strategist. Those who lean too heavily on one at the expense of the other will eventually encounter a regime in which their blind spot becomes fatal. The most durable edge comes from recognising that numbers and narratives are not rivals—they are complementary lenses through which the same market reality can be seen, understood, and acted upon.

### Continuous Learning: Encourages a mindset of ongoing skill-building and technology review

The competitive half-life of knowledge in markets has never been shorter. A trading approach that yields consistent returns today can be obsolete within months if left unexamined, eroded by shifts in technology, regulation, liquidity flows, and the evolving behaviour of other market participants. The myth that once an algorithm is "working" it can be left untouched is one of the most dangerous misconceptions in quantitative trading. In truth, *the edge lies not in the code as it exists today, but in the capacity of its creator to keep sharpening it tomorrow.* This is not a matter of tinkering for tinkering's sake, but of recognising that the market is a moving target and your methods must evolve at least as fast as the environment in which they operate.

Consider the trajectory of machine learning in trading over the past decade. In 2013, gradient boosting frameworks like XGBoost represented the cutting edge of predictive modelling for financial signals. Today, these same methods are considered foundational—still useful, but no longer a differentiator. Deep learning architectures, transformers, reinforcement learning, and hybrid statistical–machine learning pipelines have since emerged, not necessarily to replace older tools, but to expand the palette of possibilities. The trader who has not revisited their modelling choices in years risks being leapfrogged by competitors who integrate newer techniques capable of capturing non-linear relationships, adapting to structural breaks, and processing alternative datasets at scale. This dynamic does not mean adopting every novelty; it means maintaining enough technical fluency to evaluate whether a tool solves a problem you actually have.

The same principle applies to market microstructure. Execution algorithms optimised for a particular liquidity regime can underperform dramatically when tick sizes change, order book depth thins, or volatility compresses. A trader who never re-examines execution models may attribute a performance decline to "bad luck" when in reality their assumptions about slippage, spread cost, and fill probability have quietly drifted out of sync with present conditions. This is why continuous learning is not confined to the intellectual realm; it must extend into the habit of empirically checking whether your real-world results still match your theoretical expectations. If they don't, either the market has changed or you have—perhaps both.

One of the most underappreciated aspects of continuous improvement is skill decay. Programming languages evolve, libraries deprecate functions, and best practices shift. A Python developer who last studied vectorised data handling five years ago may still produce functioning code, but it is unlikely to be optimal in terms of efficiency or maintainability. Worse, gaps accumulate invisibly: the developer may not realise that a tool like NumPy or pandas has added capabilities that would make their existing workflow simpler and faster. By regularly revisiting core technical skills, traders not only improve their existing systems but also keep their problem-solving vocabulary rich enough to respond creatively when a new opportunity or challenge emerges.

This habit of renewal also guards against what might be called *edge ossification*—the slow calcification of strategies around assumptions that no longer hold. For example, a strategy built in an era of low-frequency economic data releases may become vulnerable in a world where alternative datasets update intraday and drive rapid repricing. A trader who invests in continuous learning will not only notice such shifts sooner but will also have the mental agility and toolkit breadth to reframe their model accordingly. The cost of adaptation is far lower when you are already in the habit of learning than when you are forced into it by a sudden drawdown.

Critically, continuous learning in trading is not just about technical skill but also about mental models. The best practitioners cultivate a library of frameworks for thinking about uncertainty, risk, and complex systems. They read beyond finance—drawing on behavioural science, network theory, and even fields like epidemiology—to recognise patterns of contagion, feedback loops, and regime shifts. By cross-training their minds in this way, they avoid the intellectual trap of treating markets as a closed system with a fixed set of rules. Instead, they see it as an adaptive ecosystem in which signals, players, and incentives constantly co-evolve.

Some traders resist the idea of regular skill and technology reviews, citing the risk of "overfitting to novelty." Indeed, the temptation to chase every new data source or modelling fad is real. The antidote is a disciplined evaluation process: any potential addition to your toolkit should be tested against both historical performance and a well-articulated hypothesis about *why* it might work now. Continuous learning is not the same as perpetual change; it is about keeping your intellectual inventory updated so you can act decisively when evidence supports it, rather than from a place of fear of missing out.

Technology itself can be harnessed to support the learning process. Automated monitoring systems can alert you when strategy metrics drift outside defined thresholds, prompting a review. Codebases can be version-controlled to document not just changes, but the rationale behind them—building an institutional memory that aids future decision-making. Data pipelines can be instrumented to detect anomalies in input quality, ensuring that "garbage in, garbage out" failures are caught before they corrupt live performance. These measures turn learning from a sporadic activity into a continuous, embedded function of your trading operation.

Perhaps the most important mindset shift is to see continuous learning not as a burden but as the true source of resilience. The trader who clings to a static view of their edge is implicitly betting that the market will not change faster than they can react. The trader who invests in perpetual skill-building and system review is betting on themselves—their capacity to adapt, integrate new insights, and reconfigure their approach before circumstances force the issue. In a domain where certainty is illusory and change is constant, that is the only bet that compounds over time.

When viewed this way, continuous learning is not a "best practice" or a nice-to-have. It is the price of survival in an environment where the landscape shifts beneath your feet. Algorithms may execute trades without fatigue, but the responsibility for ensuring they remain relevant rests entirely with their human creators. And the only way to meet that responsibility is to stay in motion—not blindly chasing every passing trend, but deliberately, systematically expanding your capacity to see, understand, and act on the next set of challenges before they arrive.

### Staying Ahead Without Chasing Trends: Provides principles for adopting new tools only when they serve clear strategic needs

The most dangerous form of obsolescence in trading is not technological backwardness—it is the compulsive adoption of new tools without understanding whether they actually serve your edge. In modern markets, the rate of innovation is so relentless that traders can find themselves in a perpetual state of "upgrade," chasing novelty with the same urgency as they once chased price momentum. Vendors, thought leaders, and social media feeds trumpet the "next big thing" in data, modelling, or infrastructure, and the subtle pressure to stay current can blur the line between strategic enhancement and reactive distraction. The paradox is that *staying ahead* often means slowing down enough to ensure you are not merely being pulled along by the current of hype.

At the heart of disciplined tool adoption is the principle that every addition to your arsenal should be traceable to a clearly articulated problem or opportunity. A trader who integrates a new sentiment analysis API simply because it's trending may end up complicating their signal pipeline without improving predictive accuracy. By contrast, one who identifies that their existing model underperforms during sudden narrative shifts—and tests sentiment features as a targeted solution—is far more likely to extract durable value. This framing turns technology from a shiny object into a surgical instrument, deployed precisely where the edge is weakest or the upside is most compelling.

There is an economic dimension to this discipline as well. Every new tool carries not just an upfront cost but an ongoing maintenance burden. Machine learning frameworks must be updated, API integrations monitored for changes, datasets cleaned and reconciled. Each layer of complexity increases the operational surface area for errors and the cognitive load required to manage them. Without a filtering mechanism based on strategic fit, traders risk creating systems so entangled with auxiliary tools that diagnosing performance issues becomes a forensic exercise. In such cases, the supposed "innovation" has actually reduced agility rather than enhanced it.

The allure of trend-chasing is amplified by the success stories that circulate in the trading community—often stripped of their operational context. A hedge fund announces that it has incorporated satellite imagery into crop yield forecasts, and suddenly dozens of smaller firms rush to explore similar datasets, forgetting that the fund in question also has the resources to process terabytes of imagery, hire domain experts, and run extensive validation. For a smaller operation, the same dataset may prove more of a drain than a boon. This asymmetry underscores the need for a clear-eyed assessment of your own scale, capabilities, and goals before adopting a tool simply because it worked for someone else.

One practical safeguard is to require a pre-adoption thesis for every major addition to your toolkit. This document should state the specific hypothesis, the intended integration point within your system, and the metrics by which success will be judged. Such discipline forces you to articulate whether the new tool fills a genuine gap or merely adds to the noise. It also creates a benchmark for post-adoption review—if six months in, the tool has not delivered measurable improvement in the defined area, the case for decommissioning it is strong. This form of strategic hygiene not only limits wasted investment but also reinforces a culture of intentionality over impulsiveness.

Crucially, avoiding trend-chasing does not mean rejecting innovation. Some of the most transformative improvements to trading systems come from timely adoption of new methods—often before they become mainstream. The difference is that such adoption is driven by a clear understanding of the strategic value, not by fear of being left behind. A trader who recognises that their execution engine suffers from predictable slippage in illiquid markets might explore reinforcement learning-based order placement not because it is fashionable, but because it directly addresses a measurable weakness. Here, novelty is a means to an end, not an end in itself.

Psychology plays an important role in this discipline. The human tendency toward "loss aversion" can manifest as an anxiety about missing out on a tool that competitors might use to gain an advantage. This fear can be exacerbated in public or social contexts, where traders signal their sophistication by showcasing the bleeding edge of their tech stack. Resisting this pressure requires the confidence to judge readiness by internal performance metrics rather than external signalling. The trader grounded in their own strategic roadmap can watch a trend unfold and still choose not to engage—knowing that their competitive advantage lies in precision, not breadth.

Even when a tool passes the strategic relevance test, timing matters. Early adoption can confer an advantage, but it also exposes you to higher uncertainty in terms of stability, support, and real-world performance. Conversely, waiting until a tool has matured may mean missing the initial window of outperformance, but reduces the risk of building on an unstable foundation. The optimal approach is rarely dictated by ideology—it is a calculated trade-off between the potential edge gained and the operational risk absorbed.

Case studies of failed trend-chasing are instructive. The sudden surge of interest in blockchain analytics for equity markets in the late 2010s saw firms investing heavily in crypto-derived transaction graphs, only to discover that the data had minimal predictive power for the assets they actually traded. Similarly, the rush to integrate GPT-style large language models into every facet of market analysis in the early 2020s often led to increased noise, hallucinated outputs, and degraded decision quality—especially where guardrails and validation mechanisms were insufficient. In each case, the root cause was not the technology itself, but its misalignment with the actual drivers of the trading strategy.

In contrast, those who succeed in staying ahead without succumbing to fads operate with a constant but selective scanning process. They maintain awareness of emerging tools and techniques, but they evaluate them through the lens of their own system's architecture, objectives, and risk tolerance. This filtering is not passive; it requires the intellectual humility to recognise that not every innovation is meant for you, combined with the intellectual ambition to integrate the few that truly can enhance your edge.

Ultimately, the principle is simple but demanding: *adopt when ready, not when prompted by the market's chatter*. This requires a mature understanding of your own competitive strengths, a willingness to defer adoption until evidence justifies it, and the operational discipline to manage each new component as part of a coherent, evolving system. In doing so, you not only protect yourself from the whiplash of perpetual upgrading but also preserve the clarity and stability that are prerequisites for sustained performance in markets that reward patience as much as they do speed.

# Chapter 11
# Your Personal Market Lab

The most enduring edge in markets is rarely found in exclusive data feeds, proprietary models, or the latest computational horsepower. Instead, it lies in the capacity to learn faster and more accurately than competitors. Yet, even in today's algorithmic age, many traders treat their strategies as if they were finished products—rigid frameworks to deploy until failure forces a reckoning. This is the mindset of a manufacturer, not a scientist. A trader who assumes their work ends once a strategy goes live is, in effect, outsourcing their education to the market, often through losses. By contrast, the most resilient practitioners construct their approach as a living laboratory, where every execution—profit or loss—is a datapoint contributing to a larger, evolving body of knowledge. Here, trading and testing are inseparable acts.

Adopting a scientific mindset reframes market engagement as a series of controlled experiments. Each position is not simply an attempt to capture profit, but a probe designed to test a hypothesis: Does this signal still behave as it did in backtests? How materially does execution latency affect fills in this instrument? Are certain indicators losing predictive power under a new macro regime? Structuring strategy deployment in this way extracts maximum information from every trade, irrespective of immediate outcome. This demands more than statistical diligence; it requires intellectual humility, a willingness to treat all market beliefs as provisional, and the discipline to revise them in light of evidence.

The idea of a personal market lab extends beyond individual trades to the architecture of your entire trading process. A system that only supports production strategies while excluding small-scale experiments is inherently fragile—it constrains exploration. In a mature operation, experimental trades run alongside proven strategies at carefully calibrated sizes. This creates a portfolio not just of positions but of ideas, each competing for capital and attention based on measurable performance. The aim is not to discover a single perfect model, but to maintain a dynamic pipeline of candidates ready to scale as conditions evolve or legacy strategies falter.

Central to this approach is the construction of a rigorous feedback loop. Markets offer feedback incessantly, but without a structured process to capture and interpret it, insights dissipate amid the noise. A disciplined trader treats daily activity as raw material for learning: orders and fills are logged with full metadata, slippage patterns are scrutinised across varying conditions, and signal performance is dissected to distinguish fleeting deviations from structural decay. The feedback loop is not just a technical tool—it is a cultural practice, training the mind to regard each day as a research session rather than a binary win-or-loss evaluation.

Equally important, though often neglected, is maintaining a strategy archive. This is no graveyard for failed experiments; it is a living record of intellectual evolution. Every past strategy—retired due to underperformance, obsolescence, or strategic misalignment—contains insights for future improvement. Archiving code, parameters, test data, and post-mortem analysis prevents the costly repetition of disproven ideas, while allowing rapid resurrection of concepts that may regain relevance in new regimes. In effect, the archive functions as the institutional memory of your trading practice, preserving lessons that might otherwise fade with time.

The disciplined experimenter also recognises that capital allocation in the lab should be asymmetric. Small bets on high-upside ideas allow exploration of emerging opportunities without threatening the integrity of the core portfolio. Minimal exposure to exploratory trades buys optionality—the chance to capture edges before they become obvious to the market—while mitigating the high failure rate inherent to innovation. In this way, the fear of error becomes a manageable cost of doing business, encouraging more frequent and bolder experimentation.

Philosophically, the personal market lab acknowledges that markets themselves are evolving laboratories—complex adaptive systems in which every participant's actions contribute to the experiment. Static strategies, like static species in biology, risk extinction. The lab mindset inoculates against this by embedding adaptation into the core process. It shifts the trader's role from that of a passive rule-follower to an active investigator, continually scanning for patterns, testing their persistence, and refining their exploitation.

Ultimately, the personal market lab is less a physical space than a disciplined approach to thinking and working. It demands infrastructure for rapid experimentation, meticulous record-keeping to preserve knowledge, risk controls that allow exploration without destabilising the base, and an intellectual stance that treats every trade as a contribution to a growing body of understanding. In adopting this mindset, the market transforms from a source of random outcomes into a structured environment for accelerated learning—an edge that compounds quietly and invisibly, manifesting as resilience in change and consistency amid uncertainty.

## Treating Your Strategy Like an Experiment

The most dangerous belief a trader or investor can hold is that a strategy, once designed and validated, is complete. This belief invites complacency, which in markets is indistinguishable from decay. The reality is that any trading system is a hypothesis—a provisional statement about how the world works—and hypotheses require constant testing. The idea that a strategy can be left untouched, operating on autopilot indefinitely, is seductive precisely because it absolves us of responsibility. Yet in a domain as dynamic, adversarial, and adaptive as financial markets, treating a strategy as final is the fastest route to irrelevance. To maintain an edge, one must adopt the mindset of a disciplined experimenter, approaching every trade not as a definitive verdict but as data in an ongoing inquiry.

An experimental mindset transforms how you think about the entire lifecycle of a strategy. It begins with the recognition that backtests, however sophisticated, are simulations of the past, not predictions of the future. They are controlled environments where variables can be frozen and history replayed with perfect hindsight. The live market is different: it evolves, reacts, and resists exploitation. Signals that appeared robust during development can erode rapidly when exposed to real-time order flow and changing macro conditions. The role of the trader-scientist is to treat live deployment as Phase Two of the experiment—an environment in which assumptions are stress-tested under conditions that are not only uncertain but actively shaped by the actions of others.

A genuine experimental approach requires clear definitions of what you are testing and how you will measure success. This is where many otherwise sophisticated practitioners falter. They introduce a new factor, tweak a parameter, or adjust a risk control, but fail to isolate the variable's effect. Without a disciplined design, the post-trade analysis becomes an exercise in narrative convenience—picking the explanation that feels most coherent rather than the one supported by evidence. The better approach is to define in advance the performance metrics that matter—whether that be risk-adjusted return, drawdown volatility, correlation shifts, or slippage—and to track them systematically. This transforms trading from an art of persuasion into a science of observation.

The idea is not to strip away intuition but to constrain it within a framework that resists bias. Many traders pride themselves on a 'feel for the market', but intuition, untested, is indistinguishable from superstition. In an experimental framework, intuition still matters—it often inspires the hypotheses worth testing—but the results of those tests must be allowed to overturn cherished beliefs. This is harder than it sounds because markets punish uncertainty with the same ferocity they punish overconfidence. The temptation to act on conviction without sufficient evidence is ever-present. An experimental trader learns to tolerate the discomfort of not knowing, using disciplined testing as the bridge between suspicion and action.

Real-world examples illustrate the stakes. Consider a momentum-based equity strategy that performs well in trending conditions but suffers during sharp reversals. A set-and-forget operator might accept these drawdowns as the cost of doing business, perhaps hoping the long-term trend premium will bail them out. The experimenter, by contrast, might hypothesise that drawdowns coincide with volatility spikes and design a hedging overlay triggered by intraday volatility measures. This hypothesis could be tested with historical and forward-looking data, comparing net performance against the baseline. If the results show improvement without unacceptable cost to returns, the adjustment is integrated—not as a permanent fixture, but as a working component subject to further observation. The process is iterative: hypotheses lead to tests, tests lead to refinements, and refinements generate new hypotheses.

The experimental model also shapes how failure is understood. In conventional trading culture, a failed strategy is often abandoned wholesale, written off as a bad idea. But in a scientific framework, failure is information-rich. If a breakout system stops working in small-cap equities, the experimenter asks: Has liquidity shifted? Has the structure of intraday volatility changed? Are there new participants—quant funds, HFTs—altering the microstructure in ways that invalidate prior assumptions? By dissecting failure rather than discarding it, the trader builds a map of changing market mechanics. This cumulative knowledge compounds over time, even if no single experiment produces a breakthrough.

Treating strategy development as experimentation also changes your relationship with risk. In science, an experiment is designed to minimise the cost of being wrong while maximising the clarity of the result. In markets, this means allocating only as much capital to a test as is necessary to generate statistically meaningful data. It means resisting the urge to scale a promising idea prematurely, recognising that small-sample performance can be the product of randomness rather than signal. By thinking in terms of 'experimental capital' versus 'production capital', you can protect the core of your portfolio while still exposing it to the upside of innovation.

This approach is not without tension. Some market participants argue that markets move too quickly for slow, methodical testing—that by the time you validate an idea, the edge may be gone. There is some truth here, but it underestimates the speed at which disciplined testing can be integrated into a well-designed infrastructure. The goal is not to delay action until certainty is achieved (an impossible standard), but to shorten the time between idea generation and empirical feedback. Well-built systems can run multiple micro-experiments simultaneously, each probing different aspects of market behaviour. Over time, this yields a more robust strategy portfolio than one built on a handful of untested convictions.

Philosophically, the experimental mindset forces you to confront a truth that many traders would rather ignore: you are never finished. There is no moment when your strategy is perfect, no state of permanent edge. This is not a weakness but a reality of competing in an environment where your success changes the game for others, and their success changes it for you. The market is a shifting equilibrium of adaptive agents, and the only rational stance is to be adaptive yourself. The controlled test—repeated, refined, and reinterpreted—becomes the core unit of survival.

By reframing your trading as a series of structured experiments, you move from a static to a dynamic relationship with the market. You learn to see each trade as both an opportunity for profit and a source of information, each drawdown as a dataset, each anomaly as a potential new variable to investigate. Over time, this mindset builds something rarer than short-term returns: a compounding body of market knowledge, resilient to shocks, and deeply tailored to your own decision-making framework. In a competitive field where edges are fleeting, the ability to learn faster than the competition may be the only edge that truly persists.

## Building a Feedback Loop

The market delivers feedback constantly, but most participants are poor listeners. Price ticks, order flow shifts, volatility patterns, liquidity depth—all of it is a stream of information about how your strategy is interacting with the current environment. Yet without a deliberate system to capture, interpret, and act on that information, it dissipates into noise. The result is that lessons which could refine an algorithm or enhance decision-making are lost in the churn. The art of building a feedback loop lies in converting that raw, chaotic feed into structured intelligence that strengthens your trading framework over time.

A well-designed feedback loop operates on two levels: the tactical, where small adjustments can be made to improve immediate performance, and the strategic, where long-term adaptations shape the future evolution of a strategy. The first level ensures you remain responsive without being reactive; the second ensures you don't keep solving the same problems from scratch. This dual function is crucial because trading systems, however advanced, are built on assumptions that decay. What worked yesterday is not guaranteed to work tomorrow, and without a way to measure and respond to that decay, your edge will erode unnoticed.

The starting point for any effective feedback system is measurement. This seems obvious, yet many traders collect data in ways that are too superficial or too scattered to yield meaningful insight. Recording the final P&L of a trade is not enough; it tells you the outcome but not the causal chain that produced it. Instead, you need a set of metrics that capture the full anatomy of your trades: signal strength at entry, market conditions at the time, order execution quality, latency effects, intraday volatility exposure, and behaviour of the strategy under different liquidity regimes. *If you cannot map the path from decision to outcome, you cannot meaningfully improve it.*

An instructive example comes from algorithmic execution systems in equity markets. These algorithms often have built-in logic to slice large orders into smaller increments to reduce market impact. By monitoring the slippage between intended and realised execution prices, the feedback loop can detect when market microstructure changes—perhaps due to shifts in high-frequency activity or a change in dark pool behaviour—are degrading performance. With that signal in hand, the system can be recalibrated, and the new parameters can be tested in parallel against the old ones to validate improvement. This is how feedback loops create compounding value: not by avoiding every mistake, but by ensuring each mistake informs a better decision next time.

However, feedback loops can fail in two predictable ways. The first is overfitting to short-term conditions—reacting to noise rather than signal. If your strategy underperforms for two days and you immediately overhaul it, you may be responding to randomness rather than a genuine structural shift. The second failure mode is inertia—gathering vast quantities of data but doing little to integrate it into actionable refinements. The balance lies in designing thresholds and review cycles that respect statistical significance while keeping the system nimble. This is where human oversight becomes indispensable; a machine can flag deviations, but judgment is needed to decide whether those deviations are meaningful.

The most robust feedback systems are cyclical and layered. Daily market activity generates raw data, which is then processed into performance diagnostics. These diagnostics feed into a scheduled review process—weekly for short-term strategies, monthly or quarterly for longer-horizon ones—where anomalies, trends, and hypothesis-driven changes are evaluated. Those changes are then implemented experimentally, with results fed back into the same diagnostic structure. Over time, this loop becomes a self-sustaining learning engine. *The absence of such a loop doesn't just limit growth; it actively increases fragility, because weaknesses accumulate faster than they are corrected.*

A compelling case study can be seen in quantitative macro funds during the COVID-19 shock of early 2020. Many volatility-targeting strategies found themselves forced to unwind positions in a liquidity crunch, amplifying losses. Funds with mature feedback systems were able to analyse in near-real time how their execution algorithms and risk models behaved under stress, identify bottlenecks, and implement temporary overrides to prevent further forced selling. Post-event analysis then fed into a permanent reconfiguration of position-sizing logic under extreme volatility conditions. The difference between those who recovered quickly and those who did not often came down to the sophistication and discipline of their feedback loop.

Philosophically, a feedback loop embodies humility. It is an admission that your model is incomplete and your understanding provisional. This humility is not weakness; it is a competitive advantage in a domain where conditions evolve and participants adapt. By making feedback a structural feature of your trading process rather than an occasional afterthought, you reduce the role of ego in decision-making. The market stops being an adversary to outguess and becomes a collaborator in refining your methods.

Yet this humility must be paired with rigour. A feedback loop that captures every tick of data without a disciplined process for filtering, categorising, and testing becomes a self-inflicted data swamp. The point is not to drown in information but to transform it into decision-ready insight. This often requires investment in both technology—automated data capture, real-time analytics dashboards—and process—regular review meetings, cross-strategy comparisons, and controlled trials of new parameters. Without both, the loop remains incomplete.

Over time, a strong feedback loop also sharpens your sense of causality. You begin to see patterns in how your strategies respond to macro announcements, liquidity shifts, sector rotations, or microstructure anomalies. These insights can spark entirely new lines of strategy development, turning operational data into a source of innovation. The loop becomes more than a repair mechanism; it becomes a creative engine for finding fresh edges in the market.

The ultimate measure of a feedback loop's value is not simply improved returns, but reduced fragility. A strategy that learns quickly from small errors is less likely to be blindsided by large ones. By capturing the lessons embedded in daily market activity, you create a compounding process of adaptation—one that turns the inevitability of change from a threat into a source of strength. In the long run, those who listen most closely to the market's constant feedback are the ones best positioned to survive its most violent shifts.

## Archiving and Reviewing Past Strategies

Most trading losses are not the result of failing to predict the future—they are the result of failing to remember the past. Markets evolve, yes, but human behaviour within them often repeats. Mistakes recur, biases resurface, and poor ideas get recycled, sometimes disguised in new jargon. The absence of a disciplined record-keeping and review process allows these patterns to persist unnoticed. The purpose of archiving past strategies is not merely to preserve a historical record for nostalgia's sake; it is to build an institutional memory that protects you from wasting time, capital, and conviction on ideas that have already been tested and found wanting.

An effective archive is more than a spreadsheet of trades or a folder of PDFs. It is a curated repository that captures the full lifecycle of a strategy—from the initial hypothesis and rationale, through backtesting and live execution, to post-mortem evaluation. *Without the 'why' alongside the 'what', your records will be incomplete and your reviews shallow.* This depth of documentation transforms past strategies into learning assets, allowing you to revisit them with fresh analytical tools, re-examine them under new market conditions, or re-engineer them in light of technological advancements.

Consider the case of a systematic equities trader who develops a momentum model during a strong trending market. The model thrives for several quarters, but begins to underperform as volatility regimes change. Without detailed records, the trader might abandon the approach entirely, forgetting the specific factors that drove both its success and its eventual decline. Years later, when similar conditions return, the model could have been revived profitably—but without proper archiving, it is lost to memory. Conversely, without records of the drawdown phase, the same trader might unwittingly reintroduce the strategy during unfavourable conditions, repeating the same costly lesson.

The discipline of reviewing past strategies is what gives the archive its value. This is not a ceremonial process performed once a year; it is a structured, periodic assessment that treats each historical strategy as a case study. The review should address critical questions: Did the strategy fail because the market changed, because execution was poor, or because the initial hypothesis was flawed? Were there risk controls that could have salvaged it? Were there overlooked variables—liquidity shifts, sector concentration, geopolitical events—that could have been anticipated? By answering these, the review converts a static record into actionable insight.

In institutional settings, strategy review processes are often formalised. Some hedge funds require quarterly 'post-mortem' sessions where both successful and failed strategies are dissected in front of the team. This not only captures explicit learnings but also guards against survivorship bias—the tendency to remember only the winners and forget the losers. Retail traders and small teams can adopt similar practices on a more modest scale, using shared digital notebooks, annotated charts, and code repositories to maintain transparency and continuity. The key is consistency; an incomplete or sporadic archive quickly loses relevance.

One of the most underestimated benefits of a strategy archive is its role in calibrating expectations. When you can see the historical distribution of returns, the length and depth of drawdowns, and the variance in win rates across regimes, you are less likely to abandon a viable system prematurely. Equally, you are less prone to overconfidence when a strategy experiences a short burst of exceptional performance. In both cases, the archive acts as a behavioural anchor, grounding your decisions in empirical reality rather than short-term emotions.

There is also a strategic upside to archiving that goes beyond avoiding mistakes: it enables recombination. The history of innovation in finance is full of examples where old ideas were resurrected and adapted to new contexts. A pairs trading strategy that failed in its original form might become viable when combined with a volatility filter. A factor model that underperformed on equities could thrive in a commodity market with similar cyclical patterns. *Without a detailed historical record, these creative recombinations are impossible; with one, they are limited only by your ability to cross-pollinate ideas.*

Technology has made the process of archiving easier and richer. Automated logging tools can capture every trade decision, every parameter adjustment, every market condition snapshot at the time of execution. Cloud storage allows these records to be accessible across devices and collaborators. More importantly, modern data analysis platforms allow for retrospective testing: you can run an old strategy through today's data to see how it might fare under current conditions, identifying latent opportunities or confirming that the original flaws remain fatal. The archive thus becomes a living resource, not a static museum.

The philosophical dimension of archiving strategies is worth noting. It reflects a mindset that views trading as an ongoing research project rather than a sequence of bets. This mindset values intellectual honesty—the willingness to confront evidence that contradicts your beliefs—and intellectual patience, the understanding that some ideas may need to be shelved for years before their moment returns. It is a posture of respect toward your own past work, recognising that while the markets may forget, you do not have to.

The danger of not archiving is not only the repetition of personal mistakes but also the repetition of collective ones. Entire sectors of the financial industry have been caught making the same errors decades apart because institutional memory was lost—whether through staff turnover, poor documentation, or cultural aversion to revisiting failures. A well-maintained archive functions as a defence against this amnesia. It embeds the lessons of experience into the very structure of your decision-making process, ensuring that the cost of each error is paid only once.

Ultimately, the value of an archive is proportional to the seriousness with which it is maintained and the regularity with which it is consulted. A neglected archive is no better than none at all; a living one becomes an indispensable edge. By keeping meticulous records and returning to them with disciplined curiosity, you transform past strategies from relics into resources. In doing so, you not only protect yourself from the pitfalls of forgetfulness but also open the door to opportunities hidden in the patterns of your own trading history.

## Making Small Bets on Big Ideas

The most enduring breakthroughs in markets rarely emerge from wholesale reinvention. They tend instead to arise from incremental, controlled experiments that test the viability of bold concepts without jeopardising the stability of existing success. The paradox is that the largest leaps in performance often begin as the smallest commitments of capital and risk—a reality that runs counter to the natural human urge to 'go all in' when conviction runs high. The discipline of making small bets on big ideas is, at its core, an exercise in humility: it acknowledges that even the most persuasive hypothesis can fail when confronted with live market complexity, and that survival—not just upside capture—must be the foundation of any innovative trading programme.

Small bets create a form of strategic optionality. By allocating a fraction of resources to an unproven but promising approach, you gain access to the full upside potential of the idea without exposing your core portfolio to catastrophic drawdowns should it falter. This is not about timidly tiptoeing into innovation; it is about structuring experimentation so that it is economically sustainable and psychologically tolerable. Traders who risk too much too soon on a novel idea face two dangers: the financial loss that depletes their capital and the emotional blow that can discourage future experimentation. By contrast, a well-calibrated small bet preserves both the balance sheet and the willingness to explore.

History offers numerous examples of this principle in action. The early adopters of statistical arbitrage in the 1980s, for instance, often began with minuscule allocations from their broader equity portfolios, running their models alongside traditional discretionary trades. Many of these initial models were crude by today's standards, but the risk-limited environment allowed their designers to iterate rapidly, improving algorithms without the existential pressure of large-scale losses. Over time, as evidence mounted, these small experiments evolved into primary revenue streams. The same can be seen in macro funds that tested volatility-targeting overlays during periods of policy uncertainty, or commodity desks that trialled climate-linked price models with a token portion of trading capital before deploying them more broadly.

The psychological benefit of this approach should not be underestimated. Traders are prone to confirmation bias, anchoring on the belief that the reasoning behind a new idea is sound simply because it aligns with their analytical worldview. By enforcing a small initial allocation, you create a safeguard against your own cognitive blind spots. *The market becomes the arbiter of truth, not your attachment to the theory.* This mindset encourages genuine learning: the outcome of the experiment, whether positive or negative, is treated as feedback rather than as a referendum on your competence.

Executing small bets effectively requires clarity in both design and measurement. A 'big idea' should be defined in concrete, testable terms: what specific edge does it propose to exploit, under what conditions, and with which instruments? The corresponding 'small bet' must be sized so that a complete loss of the allocation has no material impact on portfolio viability. This is not a vague notion of 'keeping it small'—it demands a deliberate calculation of risk contribution relative to the rest of the book. For systematic traders, this might involve running the new strategy in parallel to live systems within a segregated risk bucket; for discretionary managers, it could mean establishing tight loss thresholds and pre-defined review dates.

There is also an important cultural dimension, particularly in team-based trading environments. If small bets are to flourish, they must be legitimised within the organisation's decision-making culture. Too often, experimental strategies are either starved of resources because they do not yet contribute meaningfully to returns, or they are pressured to scale prematurely to 'prove their worth'. Both tendencies undermine the integrity of the testing process. The healthiest environments treat small bets as a portfolio of research projects, each with its own timeline and evaluation metrics, shielded from the demands of immediate commercial performance.

Critics sometimes argue that an overly cautious approach to deploying new ideas risks missing windows of opportunity. There is truth in this—markets can move swiftly, and a concept that is valuable today may be obsolete tomorrow. However, this is not an argument against starting small; it is an argument for designing experiments that are fast to execute and easy to scale. A small bet does not have to mean a slow bet. With the right infrastructure, a promising result can be scaled to meaningful size in days or weeks, allowing you to capture the opportunity while still respecting the discipline of controlled risk.

From a philosophical standpoint, the practice of making small bets on big ideas aligns with a Bayesian worldview. Every strategy begins as a probability estimate—an informed guess based on available evidence. By committing a modest stake, you are effectively buying more data to refine that probability. If the results shift your confidence upwards, you can increase allocation; if they shift it downwards, you can withdraw without having paid an intolerable price. Over a long horizon, this iterative process compounds your understanding of the market in a way that pure theoretical modelling cannot match.

The discipline also mitigates one of the most insidious threats in professional trading: strategic inertia. When a portfolio is dominated by proven, stable strategies, there is a tendency to avoid introducing anything that might disturb the equilibrium. This creates vulnerability to regime change, as once-dominant edges decay without replacements in the pipeline. Small bets act as a continuous renewal mechanism, seeding the portfolio with potential successors long before they are urgently needed. In this way, experimentation becomes a core component of resilience, not an optional sideline.

The broader lesson is that innovation and preservation are not mutually exclusive aims. The most sophisticated trading operations are not those that chase novelty at every turn, nor those that cling rigidly to legacy methods—they are those that maintain a dynamic balance, using small, deliberate exposures to explore the frontiers of what might work next. *The size of the stake is not a reflection of the size of the idea; it is a reflection of your respect for uncertainty.* In practice, this means that your most transformative strategies may begin life almost invisibly, running in the background, quietly collecting data until they are ready to step into the spotlight.

By institutionalising the practice of making small bets on big ideas, you create a portfolio that is not only positioned for current conditions but is constantly preparing for what comes next. This approach protects you from the complacency that can settle over even the most successful operations, while giving you a structured pathway to integrate innovation without destabilising your core. In the unpredictable theatre of markets, that balance of boldness and restraint is not merely prudent—it is a long-term competitive advantage.

# Chapter 12
# Outsmarting the Market Without Outsmarting Yourself

The greatest peril for a savvy market participant seldom comes directly from the market itself. More often, it emerges quietly, almost imperceptibly, as early success fosters a creeping conviction: the belief that you have finally cracked it. This sense of mastery is intoxicating, arriving just when your methods appear to perform flawlessly. Yet markets do not honour mastery as academia or a professional career might. In trading, the moment you convince yourself that complexity has been conquered is often the moment it begins to unravel. Overconfidence does not strike suddenly; it seeps in gradually, subtly adjusting assumptions, position sizes, and tolerance for risk. The danger lies not in making worse decisions overnight, but in ceasing to question whether your decisions still align with the realities you face.

Modern algorithmic trading, with its sleek dashboards and precise metrics, can exacerbate this trap. Algorithms produce numbers that seem to confirm skill with scientific exactitude. Yet the truth is far more fragile. Market success is never the product of code alone; it emerges from the interplay between model, market regime, and the trader's discipline in managing both. When gains are attributed solely to intellectual superiority, it becomes easy to overlook external factors—liquidity conditions, volatility regimes, macroeconomic backdrops—that may have contributed just as much to your results. The confidence of "I am smarter now" is often a distortion, created by temporary alignment between your methods and the market's current behaviour.

The remedy lies in reframing success not as a destination, but as a continual process of adaptation. Think of it less as a sprinter chasing immediate gratification and more as a long-distance runner pacing themselves through an unpredictable terrain. Quick wins are seductive—they provide immediate validation, social proof, and the impetus to scale positions—but they rarely predict future durability. Strategies that prosper in one market phase can collapse in the next, and the speed at which algorithmic edges erode today is unprecedented. True skill is measured not by exploiting fleeting inefficiencies, but by maintaining systems that endure across the spectrum of possible market conditions, including those yet unseen.

The advantage of sustained discipline over opportunistic bursts is evident in the records of enduring trading operations. These firms and individuals often report modest, compounding returns, punctuated by occasional drawdowns. Their brilliance lies not in spectacular gains but in survivability. The lesson is subtle: risk must be calibrated to ensure longevity. In practice, this often means sacrificing some potential upside today to remain in the game tomorrow. The gravest danger is not a dramatic loss, but a series of small, unnoticed decisions that erode your time horizon.

Recognising when to pause—or to step away entirely—is a hallmark of professional maturity. This is not resignation; it is strategic withdrawal. Market regimes shift, personal circumstances evolve, and cognitive fatigue can erode judgment in ways that are easy to overlook. Knowing when your edge is dulled is as critical as identifying a trade setup. Pausing allows you to reset, reassess, and preserve both financial and psychological capital for when conditions once again suit your methods. Many skilled traders erode their advantage not through spectacular mistakes, but through the slow accumulation of suboptimal trades taken from habit or impatience. A disciplined pause can be the difference between sustained participation and permanent exit.

Success in algorithmic trading must also be measured beyond simple returns. Gains are lagging indicators; they do not necessarily reveal whether your process is sound, your risk managed, or your strategy sustainable. Evaluating performance through the lens of process quality and resilience reframes the question from "Did I make money?" to "Did I make prudent decisions given the conditions and information available?" This approach does not lower standards—it prioritises metrics that genuinely predict long-term survival. Focusing on process creates a system that can learn from losses and compound insights from wins without being distorted by the inherent randomness of short-term outcomes.

The core principle of this chapter is deceptively simple: the discipline that gets you into the market is rarely the same discipline that keeps you there. Avoiding the "I'm smarter now" trap requires an active commitment to humility, even when performance appears flawless. Playing the long game demands resisting short-term validation in favour of frameworks that compound quietly over years. Knowing when to pause or quit requires courage and clarity, and redefining success requires building a trading identity not hostage to the most recent trade. Combined, these principles are more than protective measures—they form the foundation of an enduring edge. Ultimately, the true art of outsmarting the market lies in ensuring that, along the way, you never lose the capacity to outsmart yourself.

## Avoiding the 'I'm Smarter Now' Trap: Warns against overconfidence once early success arrives

The market has an unkind way of flattering you just before it humbles you. Few experiences in trading are as dangerous as the first stretch of clear, tangible success—those months when the metrics are in your favour, drawdowns seem to shrink, and you can almost believe that you've finally cracked the code. Early gains are intoxicating not simply because they add to your capital, but because they seem to confirm your intellectual worth. In that moment, *your mind subtly shifts from questioning the market to believing the market is finally confirming you*. It's a seduction as old as speculation itself, yet its modern form is sharper: algorithms, backtests, and performance dashboards feed you precise, data-backed reinforcement that you are indeed "smarter now." The danger is that the very confidence you think is empowering you is, in reality, loosening the guardrails that kept you disciplined.

Overconfidence in algorithmic trading does not usually appear as an obvious boast. It manifests in quieter, more insidious ways—a gradual increase in position sizes without proportionate increases in risk assessment, a casual dismissal of model variance as temporary noise, or a reduced appetite for stress-testing assumptions because the current system appears to be performing well. In human terms, you stop double-checking your blind spots because the road ahead looks clear. The problem is that markets are never as static as the confidence curve of a winning streak suggests. What worked last quarter may already be decaying, and the signs of that decay are often invisible until the drawdown is underway.

The financial history books are littered with examples of once-celebrated traders and funds undone not by lack of intelligence, but by the subtle creep of self-assurance. Long-Term Capital Management is the canonical cautionary tale: a group of Nobel laureates and world-class mathematicians whose early outperformance fostered an unshakable belief in the robustness of their models. Their eventual collapse was not due to sudden incompetence, but to overconfidence in the stability of the conditions in which their strategies thrived. They did not miscalculate the market's complexity; they misjudged their own capacity to remain objective in the face of prior success. *The "I'm smarter now" trap is not a flaw in your algorithm—it is a flaw in your perception of its invincibility.*

Psychologically, early success in trading taps into a cognitive bias known as the "illusion of control." The more your model appears to work, the more you attribute that performance to skill rather than to the unique combination of market factors that happened to align with your strategy. This bias is compounded in algorithmic contexts because the precision of data gives a false sense of permanence.

When a human discretionary trader wins on a few trades, they may still attribute some part of the outcome to chance. But when your code delivers twenty consecutive profitable trades, the narrative of skill feels unassailable. This is a dangerous distortion, because it replaces probabilistic thinking with the dangerous fiction of inevitability.

Guarding against this trap requires an explicit and deliberate separation of *skill* from *conditions*. Success should always be interrogated: was it the robustness of the system, or the market's temporary compliance, that drove these returns? One practical approach is to maintain a living record of not only what your system is doing right, but under what specific environmental conditions it is thriving. This means tracking volatility regimes, liquidity shifts, and macroeconomic catalysts alongside your algorithm's performance metrics. By mapping your success to external variables, you create a counterweight to the temptation of self-congratulation. *An honest audit of context is the best defence against the narrative of infallibility.*

There is also a strategic dimension to avoiding overconfidence: deliberately preserving an element of doubt in your own models. This is not self-sabotage, but rather the cultivation of what some professional investors call "constructive paranoia." The principle is simple—if your strategy is working, assume you have a limited window before its edge is eroded, either by market evolution or by competitors replicating it. This mindset forces you to continue innovating, stress-testing, and refining, even when the current data suggests you could simply scale up and collect the rewards. The paradox is that *by assuming your edge is perishable, you often make it more durable.*

Importantly, overconfidence can be as much about tempo as about tactics. Winning streaks can accelerate your decision-making pace, leading you to deploy capital more quickly, adjust parameters more frequently, and react to perceived opportunities with reduced deliberation. In algorithmic contexts, this often manifests in tinkering with live models mid-run, chasing a few extra basis points of return while compromising the statistical integrity of the system. The irony is that the very adjustments you believe are optimising performance are sometimes the ones introducing fragility. Learning to sit with a functioning system, resisting the urge to over-optimise at the first sign of a better outcome, is a discipline that separates sustainable operators from flash-in-the-pan performers.

The "I'm smarter now" trap also intersects with ego in subtle but profound ways. In the early stages, when you are testing, iterating, and debugging, there is a natural humility: you are acutely aware of how much you do not yet know. Early success erodes that humility not in a brash, public sense, but in the private conviction that you are no longer bound by the same constraints as others. You might not say it aloud, but you start believing you can "see" patterns others cannot. This belief can survive for months, even years, before the market delivers its reality check. The traders and firms who survive longest are not those who never feel this pride, but those who actively engineer systems—both algorithmic and behavioural—to counteract it.

One effective safeguard is to maintain parallel "shadow models" that are not used for live trading but serve as constant points of comparison. These shadow systems can help you detect whether your main strategy's outperformance is truly exceptional or merely tracking the market's current regime. If the shadow models begin to catch up, it may indicate that the edge you attributed to brilliance is actually a by-product of broader trends. This kind of comparative testing is intellectually humbling, but it is precisely that humility that sustains profitability.

In the end, avoiding the "I'm smarter now" trap is not about suppressing confidence entirely—confidence is necessary to take calculated risks and to weather inevitable drawdowns. The real task is to anchor that confidence in process rather than in outcome. Outcomes fluctuate; processes can be refined. By continually questioning the conditions under which your success arises, preserving a measure of constructive doubt, and structuring safeguards that check your own narrative, you build a resilience that transcends any single winning streak. The market will always test your systems, but the more subtle test is whether you can continue to test yourself, even when the scoreboard says you're winning.

### The Long Game vs. the Quick Win: Presents evidence for why disciplined, long-term algorithmic use beats opportunistic trading

The lure of the quick win has always been a central temptation in markets. It is immediate, emotionally satisfying, and can feel like proof that your instincts—or your model—are sharper than those of your peers. In algorithmic trading, this temptation takes a subtler form. You are not guessing blindly; you have data, backtests, and machine-driven pattern recognition telling you where the short-term opportunity lies. When a system delivers a rapid profit, the feedback loop is intoxicating: inputs, outputs, confirmation. The problem is not that these wins are meaningless—they are often the product of sound execution—but that they can seduce traders into believing the short-term edge is sustainable without the structural discipline of a long-term framework. *The market will always offer you opportunities to act quickly; the question is whether you should.*

At the heart of the distinction between long-term algorithmic discipline and opportunistic trading is the principle of statistical robustness. A long-term system is built to survive a wide range of market conditions, not just the narrow window in which a short-term tactic shines. In the same way that a bridge is designed to withstand decades of variable stress rather than a single crossing, a durable algorithm is stress-tested across multiple volatility regimes, liquidity profiles, and macroeconomic backdrops. Quick-win strategies often emerge from exploiting transient inefficiencies, but those inefficiencies tend to self-correct rapidly—especially in an environment where competing algorithms are scanning for the same anomalies. What looks like a repeatable pattern today may be arbitraged away tomorrow. Without the architecture of a longer-term approach, the opportunistic trader is left chasing the tail of a moving distribution.

Historical performance data across multiple asset classes supports this reality. Studies of fund longevity, from retail algorithmic traders to institutional quant desks, consistently show that strategies optimised for short-term exploitation tend to suffer from higher variance and shorter lifespans than those designed for stability. This is not an argument against tactical plays; rather, it is an argument against mistaking them for a complete strategy. The long-game trader understands that the statistical edge lies in compounding small, consistent gains while controlling drawdowns. It is not the size of the win but the durability of the process that matters. *An algorithm that survives and adapts over ten years will, almost inevitably, outperform one that wins spectacularly for two.*

Discipline in this context means resisting the emotional and cognitive biases that drive traders towards opportunism. Behavioural finance research highlights the "hot hand" fallacy, where recent success leads to an exaggerated expectation of continued success. For an algorithmic trader, this might mean over-weighting positions in a strategy that has produced a handful of strong recent returns, without recalibrating for whether market conditions still favour it. The disciplined long-term operator resists this by anchoring decisions to a broader system architecture, not to the immediate temptation of a single model's short-term results. This requires a mindset shift: treating each win not as validation of genius, but as another data point in a much longer series that must be evaluated in aggregate.

One of the most telling differences between long-term and opportunistic approaches lies in how they handle adversity. Quick-win strategies often collapse when their key condition—be it a volatility spike, a liquidity gap, or a pricing anomaly—disappears. Long-term systems, by contrast, are designed with drawdowns in mind. They incorporate mechanisms for scaling exposure, reallocating capital, or even going to cash when statistical triggers signal increased risk. This flexibility comes from the recognition that *survival is a performance metric in itself*. The goal is not to win every trade, but to keep the capital base intact and compounding.

There is also a competitive dimension that favours the long game. Short-term opportunities are highly visible to other algorithms operating in the same timeframes. As computational power and market access become more widespread, the half-life of a short-term edge has shrunk dramatically. A tactic that might have been viable for months a decade ago can now be arbitraged away within hours or even minutes. Long-term strategies, particularly those grounded in deeper structural inefficiencies or multi-factor models, are less vulnerable to rapid erosion because they do not rely on fleeting anomalies. They are designed to adapt in cycles, not in minutes, and this adaptability is an asset in a market where speed alone is no longer a decisive advantage.

Evidence from portfolio theory reinforces this view. The mathematics of compounding makes clear that avoiding large drawdowns has a greater effect on final wealth than achieving occasional large gains. A portfolio that compounds at a steady rate with low variance will, over time, surpass one that oscillates between windfalls and losses. The same logic applies to algorithmic strategies: the higher your volatility, the harder you have to work just to get back to break-even after a setback. This is why disciplined, long-term use of algorithms—where risk is managed at the portfolio level and individual strategies are evaluated for their contribution to overall stability—tends to produce superior results over years and decades.

None of this is to say that opportunistic trades have no place. In fact, many long-term practitioners allocate a small proportion of their capital to experimental or high-conviction tactical plays. The difference is that these are treated as satellites around a stable core, not as the core itself. They are measured, contained, and framed in the context of the broader strategy. This is a form of *controlled opportunism,* where the potential upside of a quick win is pursued without jeopardising the integrity of the long-term plan. The danger comes when the tail starts to wag the dog—when quick wins become the psychological centre of the operation, displacing the steady grind of disciplined execution.

From a philosophical standpoint, the preference for the long game over the quick win reflects a deeper alignment with the nature of markets themselves. Markets are complex adaptive systems; they evolve in ways that are partially predictable over longer horizons but highly chaotic in the short term. Long-term strategies leverage the aspects of market behaviour that are rooted in structural forces—capital flows, macroeconomic cycles, regulatory shifts—while opportunistic trades attempt to navigate the noise. It is not that the noise cannot be profitable, but that building an enduring edge within it is exceptionally difficult. The trader who builds on structure has a foundation; the one who builds on noise has a balancing act.

The disciplined long-term approach also fosters a different relationship with the concept of "being right." In opportunistic trading, correctness is measured in immediate profit and loss, which creates a fragile identity tied to recent outcomes. In the long game, correctness is defined by adherence to process and the integrity of the statistical model. This detachment from short-term results reduces the emotional turbulence that often derails traders, allowing them to make adjustments based on data rather than on fear or euphoria.

Ultimately, the evidence in favour of disciplined, long-term algorithmic use over opportunistic trading rests on three pillars: statistical robustness, adaptability, and psychological stability. Quick wins may dazzle, but they rarely compound into lasting wealth without the scaffolding of a broader strategy. Long-term discipline allows for the occasional tactical strike without losing sight of the bigger picture. The real victory in markets is not in winning fast—it is in winning for as long as possible, and in a way that can be sustained through the inevitable shifts in conditions. The long game is not just a safer bet; it is the only one that can stand the test of both time and competition.

### Knowing When to Pause or Quit: Explains the value of stepping back when market or personal conditions shift

In trading—algorithmic or otherwise—few skills are as undervalued as the ability to stop. The culture of markets rewards activity: constant analysis, continual position-taking, and an implicit belief that standing still is a waste of opportunity. Yet, in reality, knowing when to pause or even walk away is a hallmark of strategic maturity. *Every trader's edge is conditional,* and those conditions can and will change. When they do, the costliest mistake is often not misjudging the market's next move, but failing to recognise when your own framework is no longer suited to the environment.

The market is not a static puzzle waiting to be solved once; it is a shifting ecosystem with evolving participants, technologies, and rules. An algorithm calibrated to thrive in a trending, high-liquidity regime may find itself haemorrhaging capital in a range-bound, low-volatility phase. Continuing to run it under the belief that it will "come back" is not persistence—it is negligence disguised as faith. The capacity to step back, shut down an underperforming system, and reassess is not a concession of defeat; it is an act of preservation. *Capital preserved is optionality preserved.*

Historical examples illustrate how even sophisticated market participants have suffered from the inability to pause. Long-Term Capital Management in the late 1990s was staffed by some of the sharpest minds in finance, including Nobel laureates. Yet their models, finely tuned to a specific set of market correlations, failed catastrophically when those correlations broke down during a liquidity crisis. Instead of reducing exposure early, they doubled down, assuming a reversion to the mean that never came. The result was not just loss, but total collapse. The lesson is not that their models were inherently flawed—they had been highly profitable for years—but that their refusal to step back in the face of changing conditions left them without the flexibility to recover.

There are two primary triggers that should prompt a pause: shifts in market structure and shifts in personal capability. Market structure shifts can be macro in scale, such as regulatory changes, geopolitical shocks, or technological advancements that alter the speed and nature of trading. They can also be micro, like a new class of competing algorithms eroding your edge or liquidity drying up in your preferred instruments. Personal capability shifts are less discussed but equally important: changes in your available time, cognitive bandwidth, risk tolerance, or financial resilience can all impact your ability to manage a strategy effectively. Ignoring these personal constraints under the guise of professionalism can lead to decision fatigue, unforced errors, and compromised judgement.

Pausing is not the same as abandoning ambition. In fact, a well-timed pause can create the space necessary for creative and technical breakthroughs. When you stop executing trades, you free cognitive and emotional resources to evaluate historical performance data, run simulations under updated market conditions, and explore entirely new strategy frameworks. A trader in motion is often too consumed by daily signals and execution demands to see the structural weaknesses in their approach. The act of stopping interrupts this bias towards action and allows for strategic reflection—much like an engineer halting a production line to diagnose a fault before it causes systemic damage.

Quitting, however, is a different category of decision. Whereas pausing implies an intention to resume, quitting means recognising that a strategy, or even your involvement in a particular market segment, no longer serves your broader objectives. This is perhaps the hardest choice for experienced traders because it challenges identity. If you have spent years refining a model, the sunk-cost fallacy exerts powerful pressure to keep it alive. Yet, from a rational standpoint, sunk costs are irrelevant; only forward-looking risk-reward matters. *If the expected value of continuing is negative and unlikely to turn positive under foreseeable conditions, quitting is not failure—it is optimisation.*

From an algorithmic perspective, both pausing and quitting benefit from being encoded as formal decision rules rather than ad hoc reactions. For example, you might implement drawdown thresholds that trigger a mandatory review period or establish volatility filters that, when breached, suspend trading until conditions stabilise. This removes ego from the decision and frames it as a predefined risk management protocol. Many of the most successful quant funds operate with strict "circuit breakers" not because they lack confidence in their models, but because they understand the compounding cost of operating in adverse conditions.

There is also a psychological dividend in knowing when to stop. Trading, particularly when automated systems are involved, can create an illusion of detachment—your algorithm is working while you sleep, so the stress is supposedly lower. In reality, the stakes remain the same, and prolonged drawdowns or unexpected losses still erode mental resilience. A strategic pause gives you room to reset, preventing a gradual slide into cognitive bias or overconfidence driven by the need to "win it back." This discipline is especially important in protecting against the gambler's fallacy, where each loss increases the perceived probability of an imminent recovery, leading to reckless scaling.

The capacity to step back also aligns with the philosophy of anti-fragility. Systems that endure over time are not those that operate at maximum output in all conditions, but those that adapt by contracting during stress and expanding when the environment is favourable. By pausing or quitting strategically, you introduce flexibility into your trading ecosystem, allowing it to absorb shocks rather than break under them. This adaptability is especially valuable in an era where the speed of market evolution means yesterday's advantage can become today's liability almost overnight.

Ultimately, the decision to pause or quit is less about forecasting the future perfectly than about recognising when your current configuration—both technical and personal—is misaligned with reality. The discipline lies in admitting that markets owe you nothing, and that continuing to operate without edge is an active choice to incur risk without commensurate reward. In that light, stepping back is not retreat but redeployment: a deliberate move to preserve resources, recalibrate perspective, and position yourself for a time when conditions once again tilt in your favour. The best traders are not those who trade the most, but those who know exactly when not to trade at all.

### Redefining Success: Encourages measuring success by process quality and resilience, not just returns

The popular imagination reduces trading success to a single metric: profit. A year is "good" if it ends with double-digit returns and "bad" if it closes in the red. Yet this narrow definition obscures the deeper truth about market mastery. *True success is not about a snapshot of returns, but about the repeatability, adaptability, and integrity of the process that generates them.* A system that produces a windfall in one market cycle but collapses in the next is not a triumph—it is a temporary coincidence, one that often leaves the trader worse off in the long run because it reinforces flawed habits.

In algorithmic trading, returns are an outcome, not a compass. They tell you how you fared, but not whether your methods were sound, your risk controls appropriate, or your strategy resilient under varied conditions. A system can be profitable through sheer luck—catching an anomalous trend, benefiting from a mispriced instrument, or operating in a rare window of volatility alignment. Without understanding *why* those returns were achieved and whether they can be replicated, you are building on shifting sand. Measuring success by process quality shifts the focus from celebrating short-term gains to cultivating sustainable edge.

Consider two traders. The first delivers a 40% annual return by concentrating heavily on a single highly leveraged strategy that benefits from a rare volatility spike. The second produces a steady 12% annual return using a diversified, risk-controlled approach across multiple uncorrelated models. The market will often celebrate the first trader more, but history suggests the second is more likely to survive, compound, and adapt. The first trader's performance is impressive but fragile—it depends on a specific set of market conditions that may not return for years, if ever. The second trader's approach is robust, meaning it can absorb shocks, adjust to regime shifts, and preserve capital through varied conditions. *Resilience is invisible in bull runs, but it is the deciding factor in market crises.*

Process quality can be measured in concrete terms: adherence to pre-defined rules, discipline in risk sizing, clarity in execution, and thoroughness of post-trade review. In an algorithmic context, it includes how well data is cleaned and validated before entering the model, whether parameter selection avoids overfitting, and how systematically drawdown scenarios are stress-tested. These are not glamorous aspects of trading, but they are the foundation upon which all sustainable returns are built. If your process is inconsistent, your results—no matter how good in the short term—are unsustainable.

The importance of resilience becomes even clearer when examining historical market shocks. During the 2008 financial crisis, many traders who had been riding high on years of uninterrupted gains found themselves not only unprofitable but wiped out entirely. Others, whose annual returns were modest by comparison, weathered the storm and emerged with capital intact. The difference was not foresight in predicting the crisis—it was the quality of the underlying process. Strategies built with conservative leverage, strict stop-loss protocols, and diversified execution survived not because they "outguessed" the market, but because they were structurally designed to withstand stress.

Resilience is also about the trader's own psychological endurance. Even the most technically sophisticated strategy can falter if its operator is prone to abandoning it during a drawdown or overleveraging after a lucky streak. By measuring success in terms of discipline maintained and emotional equilibrium preserved, traders ensure that they are not undermining their own edge. In practice, this might mean tracking not only return on investment, but also "return on discipline"—how consistently one adheres to rules, avoids revenge trading, or resists the temptation to override the algorithm based on gut feeling.

Focusing solely on returns can also distort decision-making incentives. If the benchmark of success is maximum profit in the shortest time, traders are incentivised to increase position sizes, take on correlated exposures, or relax risk controls to chase gains. These behaviours can temporarily inflate results but introduce catastrophic fragility. When success is instead defined as *repeatable positive expectancy under a wide range of conditions*, traders are rewarded for patience, risk moderation, and adaptability. This is why some of the most enduring trading operations evaluate performance over rolling multi-year periods rather than single quarters or years.

In algorithmic strategy development, redefining success also demands attention to model longevity. A profitable backtest means nothing if the strategy fails in live deployment due to data leakage, parameter overfitting, or behavioural changes in market participants. A resilient process involves continual validation, scenario testing, and real-world trial periods with limited capital exposure before scaling. Each of these steps may suppress immediate returns, but they dramatically increase the odds of generating sustainable ones. The most dangerous strategies are often those that look flawless in simulation but collapse when confronted with the chaotic feedback loops of live markets.

There is a philosophical dimension to this shift in perspective as well. Markets are not competitions to be "won" in a single year; they are infinite games in which the primary objective is to keep playing. By this measure, survival is the minimum threshold of success, and the capacity to learn, adapt, and preserve capital becomes the core metric. This reframing also reduces the destructive emotional cycles of euphoria and despair that come with focusing solely on profit. If you measure your worth only by returns, every drawdown feels like personal failure, and every win feels like validation—both of which distort judgement. If you measure it by process integrity and resilience, each trade, win or lose, is simply a data point in a much longer trajectory.

Real-world investors who adopt this mindset often find themselves making better decisions under pressure. They can tolerate missed opportunities because they recognise that avoiding unnecessary risk is itself a form of gain. They are less swayed by noise because they evaluate actions in terms of long-term alignment with their strategic edge. And they are more willing to pause or pivot when evidence suggests a shift in conditions, knowing that protecting the process ultimately protects the capital.

Ultimately, redefining success is an act of intellectual honesty. It is a recognition that *returns are the shadow of the process, not the process itself.* By anchoring performance evaluation in process quality and resilience, traders insulate themselves from the dangerous swings of fortune and the false confidence that short-term profits can bring. They build systems—both technical and psychological—that can endure the inevitable tests of changing markets. And in doing so, they position themselves not just to win in a single round, but to remain viable players for as long as they choose to participate.

# About the Author

Adrian Colehart writes at the intersection of markets, data, and everyday decision-making. A long-time observer of how retail investors actually behave, Adrian focuses on turning complex, quant-driven ideas into clear, usable rules that ordinary people can apply with confidence. His work emphasizes a practical creed—test small, measure honestly, iterate deliberately—while rejecting hype and guru theatrics. He has collaborated with fintech teams and independent traders, studied the psychology of risk-taking, and built simple rule-sets for personal portfolios that privilege discipline over prediction. Adrian believes the future of investing isn't about replacing judgment with machines, but about designing workflows where algorithms check our biases and accelerate the boring parts, so our attention is free for context and choices that truly matter.

www.ingramcontent.com/pod-product-compliance
Lightning Source LLC
Chambersburg PA
CBHW031338230926
51848CB00002B/295